Rob Delaney has been named the 'Funniest Person on Twitter' by Comedy Central and one of the '50 Funniest People' by *Rolling Stone*. He writes for *Vice* and *The Guardian*. This is his first book.

'WARNING: This book may cause involuntary seepage. Some funny, funny, funny, funny s*** from the most dangerous man on Twitter. The fact that he's just as funny in long form makes me want to vomit with envy'
Anthony Bourdain

'All it takes to be as funny as Rob Delaney is luck, good timing, deep compassion, reckless imaginative agility, a flawless grasp of the inner workings of language, and criminally vast quantities of mojo. What a jerk'
Teju Cole, author of *Open City*

B

BLACKFRIARS

stick. Turban. Cabbage. **Mother.** Wife. Sister. Human. Warrior. Falcon. Yardstick. Turban. Cabbage. Mother. Wife. Sister. Human. Warrior. Falcon. Yardstick. Turban. Cabbage. Mother. Wife. Sister. Human. Warrior. Falcon. Yardstick. Turban. Cabbage. Mother. Wife. Sister. Human. Warrior. Falcon. Yardstick. Turban. Cabbage. Mother. **Wife.** Sister. Human. Warrior. Falcon. Yardstick. Turban. Cabbage. Mother. Wife. Sister. Human. Warrior. Falcon. Yardstick. Turban. Cabbage. Mother. Wife. **Sister.** Human. Warrior. Falcon. Yardstick. Turban. Cabbage. Mother. Wife. Sister. Human. Warrior. Falcon. Yardstick. Turban. Cabbage. Mother. Wife. Sister. Human. Warrior. Falcon. Yardstick. Turban. Cabbage. Mother. Wife. Sister. Human. Warrior.

rob delaney

Falcon. Yardstick. Turban. Cabbage. Mother. Wife. Sister. Human. Warrior. Falcon. Yardstick. Turban. Cabbage. Mother. Wife. Sister. **Human.** Warrior. Falcon. Yardstick. Turban. Cabbage. Mother. Wife. Sister. Human. Warrior. Falcon. Yardstick. Turban. Cabbage. Mother. Wife. Sister. Human. **Warrior.** Falcon. Yardstick. Turban. Cabbage. Mother. Wife. Sister. Human. Warrior. Falcon. Yardstick. Turban. Cabbage. Mother. Wife. Sister. Human. Warrior. **Falcon.** Yardstick. Turban. Cabbage. Mother. Wife. Sister. Human. Warrior. Falcon. **Yardstick.** Turban. Cabbage. Mother. Wife. Sister. Human. Warrior. Falcon. Yardstick. Turban. Cabbage. Mother. Wife. Sister. Human. Warrior. Falcon. Yardstick. **Turban.** Cabbage. Mother. Wife. Sister. Human. Warrior. Falcon. Yardstick. Turban. **Cabbage.**

BLACKFRIARS

First published in Great Britain in 2013 by Blackfriars

A CIP catalogue record for this book
is available from the British Library.

ISBN 978-0-349-13418-5
eBook ISBN: 978-0-349-13419-2

Printed and bound in Great Britain by
Clays Ltd, St Ives plc

Papers used by Blackfriars are from well-managed forests
and other responsible sources.

MIX
Paper from
responsible sources
FSC® C104740

This imprint has no connection with The Order of Preachers (Dominicans)

Blackfriars
An imprint of
Little, Brown Book Group
100 Victoria Embankment
London EC4Y 0DY

An Hachette UK Company
www.hachette.co.uk

www.blackfriarsbooks.com

This particular copy of this book belongs to you. *Every* copy, however, belongs to my mom. Because I am dedicating it to her. I'm dedicating it to her because unless the sun incinerates the earth in the next few decades, this book will outlast me. And I want something that will be around longer than me to show that there was once a woman in Marblehead, Massachusetts, who loved her son very much and set him on his path with a beauti-fully wrought map and the fullest of tool kits. She taught him that when things are tough, one must keep on truckin'. That woman is my mom. I love her. And you would, too.

"A heart that hurts is a heart that works."

—Juliana Hatfield

contents

contents

@robdelaney I love it when someone's Twitter bio says something like "Mother. Wife. Sister. Human. Warrior. Falcon. Yardstick. Turban. Cabbage." etc. @robdelaney My niece just said "Birds live in a birdhouse & we live in a people house!" Cute, huh? Wrong; my niece is 26 & on trial for manslaughter. @robdelaney I wonder if I'll ever love anything as much as Wes Anderson loves gingham. @robdelaney Never judge a man until you've walked a mile in his shoes. Unless they're Crocs, then fuck that guy. @robdelaney You've really got to hand it to short people. Because they often can't reach it. @robdelaney My son just said he's going to write his name on our cat with a raisin. Guess I won't have to waste money on college. @robdelaney OK, think of a number. Add 7 to it. Divide it by 2. Point at it. Show it a picture of your father. Go to sleep. Omelette. @robdelaney Chinese babies must be like "Fuuuuuck…" when they realize they're gonna have to learn Chinese. @robdelaney The story of the Titanic speaks to me because I once tripped over a bag of ice at a party & then killed over 1,500 people. @robdelaney If I were a woman, when I encountered sexism I'd be like "BRB, I'm gonna go *MAKE A HUMAN* IN MY BODY LIKE A MAGICAL GOD, YOU SAD OAF." @robdelaney Just saw a fat kid at the bus stop with a violin case. It's like hey little Mozart I know that thing is filled with snacks. @robdelaney Guys calm down; squirrels invented parkour @robdelaney Cats probably wouldn't need 9 lives if they wore tiny little helmets and didn't smoke cigarettes. @robdelaney NPR head resigns after calling Tea Party "racist." Tomorrow, NASA head to resign after calling space "big." @robdelaney Just passed a guy wearing a "# 1 Dad" T-shirt. On my way home now to ask my kids what the fuck. @robdelaney Sometimes I put a dog poop in the toilet at work so the guys don't think I only went in there to cry. @robdelaney Donuts are gay bagels. @robdelaney My son just handed me a duck & a pig from his barnyard puzzle & smiled as if that made us "even" for all the food/clothing I've given him. @robdelaney @charmin my daughter was killed by a bear yesterday when she tried to offer it toilet paper you son of a bitch @robdelaney No, it's about friendship. RT @BarackObama : Is "Wind Beneath My Wings" about Bette Midler farting through a maxi-pad? @robdelaney If you bite the inside of your mouth by accident, you should be allowed to fire a shotgun at an old bus till you feel better. @robdelaney "They make their kids do WHAT?!" - Hitler, hearing about "Toddlers & Tiaras" @robdelaney THE JEWS RUN HOLLYWOOD!! Which is probably why it's a fun place to work with a lot of great restaurants. @robdelaney

introduction

In early 2009 I was in a hotel outside of Minneapolis where I'd just performed at the Joke Joint comedy club. I was on Facebook and saw that Louis C.K. had announced he'd opened a Twitter account. Like many people, I thought Twitter was for notifying people you were taking a shit at Burger King, so I avoided it. But I thought, *"Hey, if Louie's doing it, maybe I should check it out."* I started an account and posted the worst image of myself I could find as my photo. It's me standing on a beach wearing a green Speedo with horrid blue designs swirling around my tightly bunched cock and balls. People ask if I really wear that Speedo and the answer is yes, but only under my wetsuit when I swim during the winter.

One evening in the fall of 2008, I was preparing to put on my wetsuit for a swim when my friend John said, "Jesus Christ, you look awful. Let me take a picture." As I posed, my wife looked on with a sad resignation I've seen maybe two hundred times. What's funny is that we were married a few yards away from where the photo was taken, so it was doubly sad. Naturally, many people don't like that picture and they often ask me to change it. I won't.

My first tweet was "About to go onstage in Minneapolis after I finish this tuna melt and go pee." Soon after, I realized that my favorite tweets to read were the ones that made me laugh. Tweets of no informational value were the ones that made me happiest. If I wanted to know what someone did every waking moment, I would keep them in my basement, not scan their Twitter timeline.

At the time I signed up for Twitter, I was in debt and adding to it every month. I was submitting my writing to TV shows, hoping to get a job as a writer. I would consistently get replies with comments like "Great stuff!" but no show actually hired me. Other comics were publicly expressing worry about giving up their material for free on Twitter, but since nobody was paying me to do much of anything (with the exception of the SAINTLY owners of the aforementioned Joke Joint in Minneapolis, the only club in the country that would book me a couple of times a year to head-line), I figured, *Fuck it. I'll give it away for free.* I decided to show the people who were kind enough to become my Twitter follow-ers that, whether or not they necessarily thought I was funny, I had a work ethic and liked to write jokes all day, every day.

I had also cultivated a somewhat relaxed philosophy about my own intellectual property. Some years before, I'd had the good fortune to have a joke stolen from me and performed on TV by a comic I knew. I was upset at first, but then I realized that—poor etiquette aside—the guy was funny and he would've been on TV with or without my joke. I also realized that if I couldn't immediately write several more jokes to replace it, then I wasn't funny, and I had no business calling myself a co-median. So I forced myself to make a mental adjustment and I decided that the guy had done me a giant favor. And he had. I became much less precious about material. Of course I'd be "proud" of a good joke, but I knew that I just had to continue producing material.

My silent motto when people started stealing my jokes on Twitter was, "*Go ahead and take 'em, motherfucker. Here come five more.*" My goal as a comedian was to become a Delta Force operator of humor who you could throw into an empty room with nothing and he'd make something funny, and then kill people with it. This remains my goal today.

On Twitter, I try to elicit an emotional response. Usually it's laughter. Hopefully it's involuntary. I don't fault people for posting pictures of their food or just chatting back and forth with one another; that's just not my style. People come to my page to be entertained and I view it as my sworn duty to do so.

In December of 2010, a woman named Julie Grau tweeted to me, "Would you please write me a book?" I wrote back, "I'd love to," and immediately forgot about it. The next day I got an email from my friend, the author Mat Johnson, who said I might give this friendly stranger's tweet a little more attention, as she was responsible for publishing a respectable percentage of the best books being written today. I went to the bathroom in my pants, figuratively, and wrote Ms. Grau back telling her it would be my sincere pleasure to write her a book and I asked how I might go about beginning the process formally. I also told her I happened to have a show coming up in New York—I did not—if she'd like to meet and discuss further. After that email, I scrambled to book a show in New York and bought a plane ticket.

After meeting Julie and her team in New York, I returned to L.A. and my wife and I prepared to greet our first child, who was nearly done ripening in her belly. One day while I was sitting in a McDonald's parking lot, staring at a wall and contemplating fatherhood, Julie called and formally offered me a book deal. I said, "Thank you," then hung up and started crying. A few days later our son was born.

Since that moment, I've been very lucky and have gotten to work on projects with my heroes and make a living doing stand-up around the English-speaking world, including Canada. In this book I endeavor to tell you how I got to where I am now, and perhaps more important, what celebrities wear diapers to "get off" (Dancer/Actor Channing Tatum and Texas Governor Rick Perry).

Thank you for joining me, and I wish you a terrific reading experience.

I'm the Michael Phelps of taking shits at McDonald's. **@robdelaney Just forced some dogs to look at MY boner for a change.** @robdelaney My boss is like a father to me, in the sense that he's stolen money from me & called me a faggot in front of my children. **@robdelaney Living well is the best revenge. Rubbing your asshole all over someone's cellphone is pretty good too.** @robdelaney Billion dollar idea: Figure out how to pierce Mexican baby girls' ears in utero. **@robdelaney I just did the cutest little kitten sneeze! Out of my masculine adult butthole.** @robdelaney Just watched an Asian toddler make a fully functional iPhone out of a

PART I *l'enfance*

piece of cheese and some copper. **@robdelaney Whenever a Hasidic Jew sees an Amish guy from a distance I bet he gets excited, but then he's like "Oy" when they get closer.** @robdelaney If they can grow a human ear on the back of a mouse, how come they can't grow a couple clits in my armpit? Get it together, science. **@robdelaney Our daughter Jimothy just won 2nd prize at her bvTae Kwon Do tournament!! #proud #blessed #fitness** @robdelaney I'd rather have someone SHIT INTO MY HAND than hear them clip their fingernails. **@robdelaney Made my wife a "surprise" appoint-**

ment for lap band surgery. April Fools! She left me a few weeks ago. @robdelaney If your response to calls for gun control is "Should we get rid of cars too?" the answer is, for you, yes. You should not have a gun or car. @robdelaney Probably the worst thing you can do to a person is leave them a voice-mail. @robdelaney Hey #teens! What's this "Friend Zone" I keep hearing about?? Sounds fun! Can I bring my wife? She's my best friend. @robdelaney??? RT @MittRomney: It's no "Trash Hump-ers," but Ann & I still enjoyed "Spring Breakers." @robdelaney Just heard some Japanese girls say-ing a bunch of Japanese who-knows-what. Prob-ably something about how they like my jeans. @robdelaney Just found a delicious crouton in my therapist's purse! @robdelaney Imagine a shark. Terrified yet? Well you will be when I tell you that THE SHARK IS MADE OF GLUTEN!! @robdelaney I met my wife Kevin at Lilith Fair in 2004. @robdelaney I'm not crazy about tennis but I love listening to women grunt. @robdelaney Name the thing you want most in this world. Close your eyes. Breathe deeply. Inhale my hot, beefy fart. Call the police. Tiramisu. @robdelaney Domestic violence is never OK. Even at IKEA. @robdelaney "Linger" by The Cranberries is probably my favorite song about Prince Charles farting at the 1988 British Open. @robdelaney Understood. RT @Pontifex: My pas-

la curiosité

We got our first microwave when I was ten. I'm not even sure if I was warned that it was dangerous. My parents must have thought I should understand, by that age, that if something can make ice-cold water scalding hot faster than any machine in history, I shouldn't monkey with it. The microwave's primary use was to make hot water for my mom's nightly tea. It took us years to collectively figure out that a kettle was a vastly superior tool to make tea. I guess our understanding of technology evolved backward. It's not odd, I suppose, considering that my dad grew up very poor and my mom grew up in relative wealth. My dad spent a portion of his childhood in Catholic orphanages and foster homes in Boston—even though his parents were still alive—and for part of her youth, my mom's home had an elevator in it. My dad's mom wasn't terribly interested in parenting and ran around on my grandfather, disappearing for years at a time. My dad's father was very poor and wrestled with alcoholism, so sometimes his four kids—of whom my dad was the second youngest—were placed in an orphanage or foster home for a year or two. Fuck. Now that I'm a dad, I wonder how you could arrive at the decision to let your kids out of your sight like that. Physical distance between me and my son is my least favorite thing in the world.

My mom grew up in a decidedly different situation. She was the fourth of five children in a wealthy Catholic family who lived an hour north of Boston. To this day, my family spends a couple of weeks every summer at the beach house her parents bought back in the 1950s. My mom went to Catholic school from first grade all the way through her senior year at Regis College, just outside of Boston. She has a fantastic story about a nun brutally yanking her pigtails when she laughed at a friend's antics one time in first grade, the way a beautiful little girl in first grade fucking should. A friend of my uncle's, at the same school, had his ear boxed by a nun until it bled. Desks in the classroom were set up in order of the students' grades, so there was quite literally a "stupid corner." It was a phenomenal school.

When I was in sixth grade, I did not sit in the stupid corner. We didn't have one, but I wouldn't have been placed in it anyway. I loved to read, so I loved English and Social Studies. I coasted to good grades in all the other subjects. That changed in later years, when I discovered shoplifting, cigarettes, girls, and booze, and allowed my self-will a little more free reign. But just because I did well in sixth grade didn't mean I had any kind of street smarts or would be inclined to obey the rules of thermodynamics as they applied to microwave ovens.

My mom and dad had settled in Marblehead, Massachusetts, right before my third birthday. Marblehead is comprised of two peninsulas that stick out into Massachusetts Bay, about a half an hour north of Boston. I would ride my bicycle around its perimeter most days after high school. That took a little over an hour. It's tiny. But it's beautiful, has lots of trees and beaches, and is filled with white people.

I knew a microwave oven was dangerous, in theory, and that you weren't supposed to put certain things in it. I knew, for example, that metal did not belong in the microwave. But what about an egg? It seemed like you really probably shouldn't put one in there, what with the fact that an egg is totally sealed and is soft and wet in the middle and hard on the outside.

One day, after school, I decided to put an egg in the microwave and see what happened. I ceremoniously placed the egg in the center of the microwave, closed the door, and punched in one minute. Then I watched intently as a fair amount of nothing happened. I didn't want to tempt fate, so I took the apparently unchanged egg out of the microwave, set it on the counter, and tried to dream up another experiment. Then I heard a quiet humming. It was coming from the egg. The egg was humming at a very high pitch, higher than human vocal cords can replicate, like a tiny little egg-kettle. I bent down to examine the egg and listen more closely to its song. "*Eggs shouldn't hum,*" I thought. "*Is it in pain?*" Was this a fertilized egg and had I unknowingly tortured a chick and it was now screaming for death's release in its tiny prison?

I took a butter knife from a drawer and held it over the egg. I gently tapped the egg. It immediately exploded with a loud *WHOMP.* An *amazing* volume of foul-smelling scrambled egg sprayed out. Much more foulness than one solitary egg should hold. It was all over the walls and the cupboards and the ceiling. Bits of scrambled egg stuck to my face, burning me. I brushed the egg bits off, horrified and injured. I was wide-eyed and in shock at what I had wrought.

The amount of scrambled yellow matter that blew out of the egg was roughly enough to fill a large mixing bowl that you'd use to prepare cake batter. Science-wise, it was as fascinating as watching a shuttle launch or discovering that there are fish miles below the surface of the sea that produce their own light. I now knew precisely how and why it was a bad idea to microwave an egg.

I slowly sponged egg off the walls, cupboards, and ceiling. I opened the windows because it smelled disgusting—a sick, wrong smell that called to mind a hospital trash barrel. I can still re-create the smell in my mind. It smelled much, much worse than if someone farted directly into your nose and mouth. The cleaning process wasn't a panicked one; the smell was such that, even as I climbed up and stood on top of counters to clean egg bits out of the ceiling molding, I knew my parents were going to find out. As pretty as the scrambled eggs looked, the smell immediately alerted you to the fact that they'd been prepared in an unconventional manner. It fucking stank, like a dog fart in a slaughterhouse, or if an old man prepared a cottage cheese soufflé in his underpants. There was no hiding what I'd done.

Additionally, I now had two good-sized burns on my face. One on my forehead and one beside my nose. When my mom came home, I told her what had happened. I couldn't not; her home smelled like a tomb and her son had suppurating bloody wounds on his forehead and on the side of his nose. She just gave me a look that said, *"Wow, you can fuck up in ways I'd never even imagined,"* and told me not to do it again.

My wounds blistered and everyone in school asked me what had happened. I was too embarrassed to tell the truth, so I told people that my sister had thrown a potato peeler at me. Let's pause: How fucking awful and unrealistic is that as an excuse? Excuses are not my strong suit. Plus, what if she really had thrown a potato peeler at my face? Wouldn't that speak to a home-life situation that was more "embarrassing" than adolescent curiosity gone wrong? Also, my sister is, and was, one of the gentlest people I have ever met and she would never throw a napkin at someone, let alone a potato peeler.

A few days after my microwave experiment, I was sitting in class and felt a gentle *"pop"* on my forehead and hot liquid ran down my face. It was the burn on my forehead just tenderly exploding, of its own volition, on my eleven-year-old face. As the pus—filled with healing white blood cells—trickled down my face, I thought, *"I deserve this."*

ma vie avec les juifs

In Marblehead, Massachusetts, there are a lot of Jewish people doing all kinds of Jewish things all over the place. I'm Catholic, but I went to the Jewish community center for nursery school, so I witnessed much Jewish activity from an early age. I blew the shofar, ate challah, spun dreidels, and even had my penis customized in keeping with Abraham's covenant with G-d. (I omitted the "o" in that last word out of respect for my Jewish readers, even though, as a Catholic, I can write that word all day long if I want. But I don't, because I'm not a serial killer. Plus I have a family and a job.)

On my first day of nursery school at the JCC, my dad, who

grew up in Catholic orphanages and foster homes (i.e., not a Jew), accompanied me for the first hour or so. Other parents were with their kids too, to ease the transition from hiding behind Mommy's skirt to socializing with other dirty human children. The first activity our teacher, Ms. Sherry, led us in was a song to learn one another's names.

The class would sing (to the tune of "Frère Jacques"), "Where is Robby? Where is Robby?" It was then my duty to stand and sing, "Here I am! Here I am!" Which I did, beautifully I'm sure.

The class then replied with, "Very nice to meet you. Very nice to meet you. Please sit down."

After my angelic solo, they moved to a boy named Andrew.

"Where is Andrew? Where is Andrew?"

I stood up and announced to the class, "ANDREW'S DEAD." A not-dead little boy named Andrew immediately began crying and his father ran and scooped him up to protect him from any further terrifying bombshells the scary gentile interloper might decide to drop.

The reason I announced Andrew's passing was because my grandparents' dog had moved on to that big kennel in the sky a few days prior. His name was Andrew. I'd assumed Ms. Sherry was singing about him.

Today I live in Los Angeles, California, which has even more Jewish people than Marblehead. To be honest, I wouldn't even think of living somewhere that wasn't swarming with Jews.

Not long ago I leapt out of bed at about 6:30 a.m. and went

for a run in a residential part of Hollywood. When I was a few miles from my home my bowels sent an urgent cable to my brain, apologizing for the short notice and saying that they'd be emptying themselves in one minute or less; the location was up to me. I frantically searched for an alley or a dumpster I could hide behind. Nothing. Two parked cars I could crouch between? No. It would be a terrible neighborhood in which to play hide-and-seek or smoke pot surreptitiously as a teenager— no little nooks for sneaky behavior anywhere. It was particularly ill-suited for public adult shitting. The one plus—and it was a big one—was that it was so early in the morning. No one was around, in any direction. I knew that whatever horror was about to ensue, it would be over quickly. I crouched in the gutter at the end of a driveway that led to the garage of a home that actual people lived in, and shit furiously and hatefully into the street. I began to know relief.

My relief was short lived, however, because when I looked up from my pathetic al fresco bio-vandal squat, I locked eyes with a Hasidic woman who had materialized across the street. She was paralyzed by what she saw. We gazed into each other's souls and silently agreed that I was the worst person in the history of humanity and that my name belonged nowhere near the Book of Life.

la sexualité

It's easy to get fat. In fact, it's beyond easy. It's fun to do, too. When someone says something is easy as pie, I think, *"What aspect of a pie? Cooking it? That's not easy, and I know how to cook lots of things. No, Rob, they mean eating it."* It is easy to jam a tasty pie, or even a shitty pie that you bought at a gas station, right the fuck into your fattening faceblob. It's also been said that the first bite tastes the best, but the rest of them taste pretty good too.

When I was a kid, my family and I would eat every Friday night at Pizzeria Regina in Salem, Massachusetts, just one town over from Marblehead. Every other family dinner was eaten at home, so Friday was a big deal. We'd eat a pie of pizza while "Rock You Like a Hurricane" or "Eye of the Tiger" played on the jukebox (because I'd picked it), then we'd walk by a small park with a massive sculpture of Nathaniel Hawthorne seated on a throne, and go to Alden Merrell Cheesecakes, and we'd eat a pie of that, too. And indeed, it was easy.

Cheesecake. Are you shitting me? Who invented that? Probably Jesus of Nazareth. Or maybe Louis Pasteur. It makes me physically sick to think that Barack Obama won the Nobel Peace Prize, yet the name of the inventor of cheesecake isn't tattooed on Dick Cheney's face.

On one of these Friday Pie Nights, my dad and I went to the bathroom at Regina's and I saw the word "CUNT" carved into a door in huge letters. Whoever did it took their time and put real care into it. "CUNT." Not "Lisa is a cunt" or "I enjoy putting my penis in a thing called a cunt." Just "CUNT." I asked my dad what "cunt" meant and he said it was a bad word and that he'd explain it to me when I was older. I can still see him grimacing and sighing as he wrestled with how to explain that amateur woodworker's earthy carving.

Now, I agree that it's a bad word to say into a person's face if you're angry, but otherwise it'd be fair to call me a massive fan of that word. I wonder how many times a day I say it or think it. That is a question I'd like to ask God after I die. I'll call anything a cunt—a woman, a man, a child, a cup of yogurt if I drop it on the floor. It's just fun to say. Oddly, I'd never call a woman a bitch, but I'd call quite literally anyone a cunt. "Bitch" is just too gender specific and bums me out. I won't pretend that my logic makes sense.

Whenever I imagine a God that has a corporeal form, body, and voice, I imagine that Its favorite thing to do would be to field questions like, "How often did I say or think the word 'cunt' in my life?" Or "How many beers did I drink over my life, exactly?" or "Why do Orthodox Jewish women think You want them to hide their pretty hair under a wig that looks like ugly hair?" Perhaps the answer to that last question is on page one of the Talmud, but I prefer to keep a little mystery in my life—especially where Jewish women are concerned. I suppose it would be a colossal bummer if there were a God who resembled the shitty, small-minded, accountant-type God I've imagined here. Clearly Gods invented by humans like me or Michele Bachmann are a very terrible idea.

I think about fat and getting fat and being fat now that I'm married and don't drink or do drugs. I don't get high in the classical sense and I don't chase women around. So shouldn't I devote a big slice of the pie of my day to shoving food into my body, primarily through my mouth? As it enters my mouth, the taste makes my brain go *"DING DING DING! YUMMY HEADED TOWARD MY TUMMY!"* Then it has the bonus effect of slowing down my thoughts and making me feel like I'm being hugged from the inside by somebody who really loves me, unlike the terrible "people" in my life. I suppose I shouldn't eat in this manner, but keep in mind: fuck you.

My wife and I almost got into a fistfight a few nights ago

over my peanut butter consumption. Her argument is that she wants me to stay "alive" and "healthy" so I can stick around and help her raise our "son." I'm the first to admit that her argument has merit, but there's a café that sells day-old mini-cheesecakes for TWO DOLLARS four blocks from our house. So that's not an argument she can win.

One night, after eating at both Regina's and Alden Merrell Cheesecake, we went home and my dad and I sat on our front steps. We did that a lot when I was young. We'd either sit on the steps or go for long walks on the golf course that was right off the end of our street. Sometimes we'd just walk across the street and look at our house from there. My dad said it made him happy to look at our house and think about the fact that we all lived there together. It must have been a big deal for him to have his own kids with him, under the same roof every night, since he didn't grow up that way.

That particular night we were discussing a film we'd recently watched called *The Right Stuff*. I had generally enjoyed it but I was curious about one detail in the film. During one round of medical tests, the prospective astronauts were asked to provide semen samples. I knew what semen was, where it came from, and that, delivered into a woman's egg, it created human life; that much had been addressed in my science classes at school. What I didn't know was *how* semen was procured. So I asked him.

"Do they, like, squeeze it out of their balls?"

"Uh, well, not really. It's more like . . . KEN! Hi, Ken!" My dad frantically flagged down a passing car to talk to a neighbor who lived a couple streets over and was driving by.

Not long after that, I figured out how they got it by asking an older cousin. With that knowledge, one night, in seventh grade, I gathered up the courage, made sure I had some privacy, put on some Peter Gabriel, and messily jerked off with Vaseline and both of my hands, for some reason. Later I'd perfect the one-handed method, and—though I never aspired to be an astronaut—I began a lifetime of producing samples of my own.

Like many a lad, those samples were produced with the aid of nudie mags like *Playboy* and *Penthouse*, and since I was only thirteen, I resorted to theft to get them. The first time I stole a *Playboy* magazine was from a pharmacy at the end of my street. They kept their magazines and newspapers by the entrance and you paid at the register, which was at the back of the store. My plan was to take a *Playboy*, slip it inside a copy of the *Boston Globe*, and purchase the paper.

I was almost sick with nerves as I executed the insertion of the magazine into the newspaper. I could feel my heart beating in my throat. I picked it up and walked it to the back of the store to "pay" for it, confident, POSITIVE, that I was going to get caught. But the old man who worked the register just smiled and said thank you as I handed him fifty cents while stealing five bucks' worth of hot 1990s tits and ass.

I walked down the street to my house believing that a police sniper's bullet might pierce my skull at any moment. When that didn't happen, I reached my house, passed my mom in the kitchen, and stammered, "HELLO . . . I'M HOME . . . NOTHING IS OUT OF THE ORDINARY." I perused my ill-gotten gains in my bedroom and began to relax, thinking, "*I could do that again.*" And I did.

I started stealing nudie mags regularly. Then I moved on to cassettes at the local Bradlee's. I stole because I liked taking stuff that wasn't mine and not paying for it. I liked the thrill of getting away with something, of duping cashiers and security guards and being bad. It was an adventure and a gamble. Security cameras weren't what they are now, and I generally stole from smaller stores, so beyond the sideways glance, I never felt close to getting caught.

It was all very fun, and because it was fun, I liked to talk about it to my friends. And they liked to hear about it. Since I fancied myself such a good little thief, I thought it a shame to hog my God-given talents. So I decided to start a little business. I began to take orders from kids at school for specific magazines, tapes, or cigarettes, which I would then steal and bring in to school to sell to them at a "discount" from the store price.

The long arm of the law finally, and quickly, caught up with me. I don't know who snitched or what security camera caught me, but one morning I was in my bedroom getting ready to go to school. I put a couple of *Penthouse* magazines and some AC/DC and Led Zeppelin cassettes in my backpack to bring to my customers. When I went downstairs to eat breakfast, I left my backpack in the living room, and after breakfast, when I surreptitiously looked in my backpack to double check my booty, it was gone.

"Are you missing something?" my dad asked, and I froze. He said, "We know what you're doing." I got woozy and started to panic. I told him I didn't feel well. He suggested that I put my head between my knees and breathe if I needed to collect myself, but that, even if I hyperventilated, I was in big trouble. After the nausea passed, he and my mom drove me to the police station. My own dad was turning me in.

When we got to Marblehead's tiny police station, the desk sergeant buzzed us in and we were escorted to a detective's office. He had a shotgun hanging over his office door. With the progression of the day's events, it didn't seem crazy to think he might take it down and shoot me after a short speech. Instead, he told me that the police had security footage of me stealing things, and that he knew about my crime empire at school. He told me I wasn't technically under arrest, but that the MPD now had a file on me, and that if there was any further trouble, I'd be very arrested.

My parents looked on sternly, soberly, disappointed. Why wouldn't they be? Years later I found out that the detective was a family friend and that my dad had set the whole thing up. My mom had not liked the plan one bit. While I understand the argument against personally taking your kid into a police station after informing the cops of their actual—if minor—crimes, I think my dad did a good thing. My mom's punishment philosophy was to keep it "in-house" since her particular strain of advanced Catholicism put a *major* premium on privacy, so she was quite strict, but would never advocate employing outside agents. My dad, however, just thought, *"Fuck it; I don't want to live with a little thief."* And after that day, he did not.

Porno mags, cigarettes, cheesecake, shoplifting; they made me feel good from an early age. Not as good as booze ultimately would, but like a lot of adolescents (and also alcoholics-to-be), I just felt a little "off" most of the time. My favorite part of any day, back then, was when I'd flood my system with a little adrenaline, feel the buzz that came from an illicit action, like throwing a rock through the window of an abandoned house, or poring over pictures of naked women in locker rooms, who were surely alone somewhere, fantasizing about me and my acne.

le narcissisme

The worst thing I ever did in my whole life (and I've crashed cars drunk, lied to my wife about money, and I even took a shit on a guy's drum set once) is when my mother made me a cake for my thirteenth birthday, and I refused it.

When I was twelve, I loved the band Danzig. I still do. I literally—no joke—had a dream last night that Glenn Danzig visited me in a childhood friend's attic and showed me his new tattoos. I know it was a dream because these tattoos were awful and Danzig's real tattoos are one hundred percent bitchin'. But did I tell him they were awful in my dream? No, I did not. Out of respect.

I loved Danzig so much that when I realized he parted his hair on the right, I switched the part in my hair from the left to the right, retraining the hair on my head to match his. This was twenty-two years ago. My hair is still parted on the right.

I loved Danzig so much that I wrote him a letter (still at age twelve) detailing just how *much* I liked him, since I thought he would for sure want to know. I don't remember what I wrote exactly but I do remember that upon finishing the letter, I read it and noticed that I had used contractions such as "can't" and "won't."

That is not formal enough, I thought. *Glenn deserves a letter with the words fully written out. How can I expect him to read a letter sullied with such lazy slang?*

So I rewrote the letter, changing the *"can't*s" to *"can not*s" and the *"won't*s" to *"will not*s," etc., deemed it worthy of his eyes, and mailed it off. The address that I sent the letter to was procured from liner notes to their second album that was delivered to my local record store by a UPS truck that was chased by me and two friends on our bicycles, since I knew it was the release date for *"Danzig II: Lucifuge."* I watched as Jim, the potbellied (cheesecake?) and mustachioed owner of Bedrock Music, sliced open the box, exposing its evil cargo to the light. After writing the letter I probably climbed a tree with a *Sports Illustrated* swimsuit issue and wondered what Elle Macpherson's hair smelled like.

A few weeks later, I heard the mailman drop some letters through the mail slot onto the floor of our front hall. As I sifted through the bills, catalogs, and other boring adult stuff,

I came upon a letter from Van Nuys, California, with the name "Danzig" stamped in the upper left corner. I carefully unsealed it to reveal a letter from Eerie Von, Danzig's bass player. It was written with a Sharpie marker and there were some grammatical errors that suggested I hadn't needed to be so vigilant about my contraction use, but the letter's tone was kind and warm and endeared Mr. Von to me for life. He explained that Glenn couldn't possibly answer all his mail, so Eerie lent a hand sometimes. He thanked me for my enthusiasm and hoped I'd tell other people about the band. Naturally, I did, because I was at the age where I would physically sit people down and force them to listen to the songs I liked, watching their facial expressions closely as they reacted to each note.

And just in case Eerie Von's first letter didn't cement Danzig's position as the world's greatest band forever, he wrote me another one, unsolicited! Some months later I got the second letter from Von saying, essentially, "How's it going, man? Everything groovy? Still rockin' to Danzig?" Indeed I was. What a gentleman. I'm now on my third or fourth Danzig monster skull T-shirt, and when this one falls apart, I plan to get another.

At that age, my mother and I spent a lot of time together, and she paid attention to my adolescent passions, even deigning to listen to the odd Danzig ballad that I'd force upon her, conceding that it was "Yeah, nice. Sure." So, for my thirteenth birthday, she made me a Danzig birthday cake. It was magnificent and included all four members of Danzig's faces, which were easily identifiable. Glenn himself was large and on the left. Eerie Von, guitarist John Christ, and drummer Chuck Biscuits were smaller and on the right. Although her only tool was a simple chocolate cake decorator in a tube over vanilla frosting, she was able to depict delicate shadows and convey the darkness of Danzig's majesty. It was a great cake and, when she presented it to me, I became infuriated.

"Mom! Come on! Danzig shouldn't be on a cake! They're like, bad dudes! They would never be on a cake! Maybe they'd be, like, on a tombstone or a gunslinger's coat, but a cake! No way! Jeez!"

I want to cry thinking about the pain that was on her face. Here was a woman who worked full-time at an insurance agency, working very hard to support her two kids, also making sure to be extremely present in our lives—mornings, evenings, and weekends. She had worked on her masterpiece in secret, studying each band member's scowl, to make her self-proclaimed bad-ass little boy an extremely cool cake, and he hated it. And he let her *know*, like a real piece of shit. Now that I'm a parent, the idea of my children expressing displeasure at my efforts to please them makes me want to lie down on a table saw.

My mother simply smoothed off the guys' faces with a spatula and then covered the cake with chocolate sprinkles, or "jimmies" as we called them then, but which I'm now told is a racist term.

Later that night, for my official birthday celebration, my friends Rich and Matt and I saw the film *Tango and Cash*, starring Sylvester Stallone and Kurt Russell as cops who are framed for murder and then break out of prison. Then Rich and Matt slept over, our bellies full of the cake my mom had made and then remade when it failed to meet my satisfaction. To this day when I imagine having a time machine, my FIRST stop is my thirteenth birthday where I would jump up and down with excitement and hug my mom when she reveals that cake. If there was still time left on my time travel visa, only then would I go back and kill Hitler.

la honte

I stopped wetting the bed while sober at age twelve. I wet the bed while drunk until I was twenty-five years old. I first got drunk at twelve, though, so that tacked on another thirteen years of waking up wrapped in the piss-soaked sheets of beds across the United States, Canada, and France.

When I was nine, my pediatrician suggested that my bed-wetting persisted because I was a deep sleeper and that the condition would ultimately resolve itself. In the meantime, on the mornings that I had wet the bed, I'd wake up, sense what had happened, and get sad. Then I'd strip my bed down to its crinkly plastic mattress cover and trudge down to the basement, arms full of soiled sheets, praying that I didn't pass my mom, dad, or sister (who was five years younger than me, yet woke up each morning in a bone-dry bed, ready to attack the day). Then I'd throw the sheets in the washing machine with detergent and a little bleach. A framed pastel drawing I'd done depicting bright red flowers that looked like gaping, bloody grenade wounds hung over the washing machine. Then I'd go back upstairs, spray a little Lysol on the bed, put clean sheets on it, and take a shower. My parents handled the situation as best they could. They loved me.

Perhaps the most scarring bedwetting memory is when I tried to sleep over at the summer camp I attended for nine years as a kid. It was a day camp owned by the YMCA called Children's Island and it was about a mile outside of Marblehead Harbor. Every second Tuesday evening, campers' parents would visit their kids and have a picnic, then the campers would stay overnight in tents. Naturally the idea terrified me but I yearned to be a normal boy, so one day I decided to give it a shot and resolved to spend a Tuesday night on the island. My parents got some subs and sodas from Super Sub and brought my four-year-old sister along for the twenty-minute boat ride on the *New England Star*, the ferry that brought us back and forth each day. I loved riding on the bow of that boat on a choppy day and being sprayed by waves in the afternoon sun. It's entirely possible that that's the memory that will flash before my eyes when I die, it's so satisfying.

I brought my parents and sister around the tiny island that smelled of salt, wild grass, and seagull shit. I showed them my projects at the arts and crafts lodge and rocks on the island's edges that looked like whales. I think it's fair to call the situation idyllic. As the sun prepared to set, my family got ready to see me off and my parents reminded me not to drink any liquids and to make sure I "emptied the tank" before going to sleep. I bid them goodbye and waved as the boat pulled away from the island and made its way back to the mainland.

Then all the campers and counselors put on warmer clothes and meandered to the eastern edge of the island to gather around a giant campfire, sing songs, and watch the counselors do skits, which were shockingly, improbably good.

My friend Todd and I confided in each other after the fact that when Ranger Pete, the camp's nature director, sang an original song containing the phrase "The island has a mystic veil around her, pulling me so close I cannot leave," we cried.

After the campfire we found our way to our tents, with me making a pit stop at the bathroom in the main lodge, trying to squeeze out every possible drop of urine. Then I got in my tent with eight other boys and fell asleep.

Around seven the next morning, I woke up in the sleeping bag thoroughly soaked with piss. My greatest fear had come to pass. *What do I do?* I thought. *How do I escape this?* I tried to silently gather up my sleeping bag and sneak out of the tent.

"ROB PEED IN HIS SLEEPING BAG!" a boy named Liam yelled.

"No I didn't!" I responded, vibrating with fear.

"Yeah you did."

"No! I didn't."

"Why's it all wet then?"

"It isn't! If . . . would I do *this* if I'd peed in my sleeping bag?" I gathered up my sleeping bag and took the wettest area and rubbed it all over my face. Why I thought that would prove anything is beyond me; I was terrified and ashamed and I didn't know what to do. Was I shaming my own inner puppy for peeing somewhere he shouldn't have? Psychologically, it was a pretty delicious scene.

Liam was horrified and I could see that he immediately regretted calling me out because he now knew he was partially responsible for inciting a psychotic break in another kid. You could see he thought *This boy might go on a killing spree one day, so distant is reality from his sad, flailing grasp.*

I struggled through the following day's archery and sailing lessons and rode the *New England Star* home that afternoon. When my mom picked me up I told her I'd wet the bed. She was very kind to me and we drove to a laundromat to wash my sleeping bag. I guess our washing machine at home wasn't big enough for the job. I sat in the car while she brought it in to wash.

Before she got out I said, "What if somebody comes by and asks why we're washing a sleeping bag?"

"Just tell them you spilled a Coke on it," she replied.

I was *certain* that all the town folk would come down to the river's edge of the laundromat and interrogate me as to why we were washing a sleeping bag *immediately after a sleepover* so I rehearsed the Coke excuse my mom gave me over and over. I clung to her ruse like a nineteen-year-old refugee would hold her baby as she crossed a mountainous border during a snow-storm.

I imagined Old Man Carruthers approaching:

"Hi Rob, how are y—"

"I SPILLED A COKE ON IT!"

"I'm sorry?"

"I SPILLED A COKE ON IT!"

"On what? Son, are you okay?"

"It's JUST COKE! I SPILLED A COKE ON IT!!!"

"Ok, I gotta hit the road. You take care . . ." Old Man Carruthers sauntered off, mumbling, "I guess it takes all kinds . . ."

Shortly after this episode, my parents took me to the doctor to see what my options were. Option 1 was a pill I'll call "Dehydromax 5000." I hope to God this medication went the way of leeches and the lobotomy, because not only did it keep my bed dry, it also kept my mouth, throat, and eyeballs at the same moisture level as the ash at the end of a generic Russian cigarette. Eventually my blinks became audible across the dinner table, and my parents decided I should quit taking it.

Option 2, which we tried next, was a special alarm that my mom had to order from some pre-Internet catalog of horrors. I can remember the package coming in the mail, opening it up, staring at it more intently than anything I'd ever received from Santa, and thinking, "Is this the thing that will save me? Will the thing in this box help me be like other boys?"

The alarm consisted of a sensor that attached to a wire, which ran to a tiny box that emitted a terrifying shriek if it detected any moisture. It was so sensitive that even the moisture on one's finger would set it off. It slid into a pocket that my mom had sewn onto the front of a pair of my underpants; the wire ran up to the alarm, which adhered to a Velcro patch she had sewn onto the shoulder of one of my white T-shirts.

Perhaps the pee-sensor industry has since graduated to some sort of waterproof Bluetooth alarm that makes the wire superfluous, but in 1987 it was an essential component, which created a problem: The alarm was designed for children, who are usually short. I was not. In fact, I was the tallest kid in my school. Thus, the wire wasn't long enough to reach from the pocket on the front of my little underpants up to the patch on the shoulder of my shirt. So at night, when I slid into my little white cotton shame-suit, I had to hunch down as though I had terrible scoliosis and lurch over to my bed, already hating myself. Then I'd slither between the sheets and lie there, awaiting the inevitable. But since I did indeed sleep as deeply as my pediatrician had suggested, I always slept right through the alarm and had to be shaken into consciousness at ungodly hours of the morning by one of my bleary-eyed parents as I lay there in a piss-soaked bed with a shrill robot scream boring into my disoriented brain.

As I experimented with the alarm, a miraculous thing happened: My brain and bladder fused a better—if sometimes still faulty—connection simply because I was getting older, so I began to wet the bed less and less, thus freeing me of those horrible aids.

A couple of years after my experience with the alarm, I got

drunk for the first time when my friend John's older sister threw a party at their house. I drank three or four cans of Budweiser and, boy oh boy, did I like the way I felt. I remember an older guy punching me very hard in the arm when I said I didn't think *Ride the Lightning* was Metallica's best album. Another guy threw me off John's back porch into a rose bush. An adult man wearing a T-shirt with a swastika on it stuck a joint in my face and I was too afraid not to smoke it. I later recognized his face on the front page of the *Marblehead Reporter.* He was in court, in handcuffs, giving the photographer two middle fingers. He'd been arrested for spray-painting the names of concentration camps all over a temple in town.

I was drunk that night though, so none of that fazed me. I'd found a new ally of sorts, and it made things like physical pain just disappear. And that made the return of the bedwetting worth it, for a while anyway. It's funny to think that I wet the bed for slightly longer as a drunk than I did in my youth. With my wife's recent pregnancy, I learned that babies even go pee-pee inside their mommy's tummy. So I peed while sleeping from shortly after conception till age twenty-five, at which point I had a hairy chest and weighed just under two hundred pounds. Twenty-five; a silver-golden anniversary, if you will. But you shouldn't, because it's a mess.

sion for Florence & the Machine's percussive anthems has finally exceeded my love for Christ. @robdelaney If you're a guy in a tank top, do a gymnastics routine or get the fuck away from me. @robdelaney GALS: Ask ANY guy, if you don't know all the sex tips from the latest Cosmo, we are NOT interested. @robdelaney What's all the fuss about horse meat? Who gives a shit? I'll eat a horse. I'll eat a dog. I'll eat your fucking family. @robdelaney Sort of rude to kiss your husband right in front of me when I've been looking at your boobs from behind a tree for 20 minutes. @robdelaney Haven't had intercourse in a while so I'm heading down to

PART II   *la soûlerie*

the shipyard to make a bad decision. @robdelaney Not a fan of the term "MILF." When I was a #teen, we called them "yummy mummies" & left it at that. #respect #imagination #lotion @robdelaney Children give terrible gifts because they're poor. @robdelaney My cousin Denise's baby Alpo was born with no feet and a full adult penis because she drank Four Loko when she was pregnant :(@robdelaney @wolfblitzer can I spraytan my baby? @robdelaney How many spiders are in your vagina RIGHT NOW? The answer may surprise you. @robdelaney Just saw an unbelievably beautiful woman in the park. I wonder how many cows her father would give me to marry her. **@robdelaney Why are blood oranges the only "blood" fruit? Why not blood bananas? Who wouldn't like to slurp down a nice ripe blood banana?** @robdelaney I need to get my shit together. It's in little piles in my kitchen & then there's some more in my wife's closet. **@robdelaney If I ever build my own house, I'm putting a toilet right in front of the refrigerator.** @robdelaney I bet if Amy Winehouse had changed her name to Amy Lemonadehouse, she'd still be alive today. **@robdelaney The hour I lose from daylight savings time will now be multiplied by 6 as I try to change the time on the clock in my car.** @robdelaney Pretty cool that the letters "B.J." stand for the two greatest things in the world: beef jerky & Billy Joel. **@robdelaney It's like taking candy from a baby - A GOOD IDEA IF YOU DON'T WANT THE BABY TO LOSE ITS FEET TO DIABETES BEFORE IT TURNS ONE.** @robdelaney Just saw a guy on rollerblades. He was surprisingly sweat-free for having presumably "bladed" here from 1991. **@robdelaney "Parodies" or homages or whatever the fuck they are of the "Got milk?" ads are worse than AIDS + 9/11 + a 3rd thing you personally hate.** @robdelaney If you ask someone out and they say no, try it again in a few minutes wearing sunglasses and smoking a ciga-

l'excès

I don't think my problems with drinking are rooted in anything too fascinating, other than genetics and a bottomless appetite for life. As a kid of Irish Catholic heritage born in Boston, Massachusetts, my extended family had a standard ratio of roughly fifty-fifty for gutter drunks versus relatively normal people where alcohol and drugs were concerned.

I first got drunk at age twelve. Someone finally put me to bed when I was deemed too fucked up to hang out anymore. I'm aware now that it was an empirically terrible night, but the feeling alcohol gave me was so magical that it outweighed the night's lousier aspects and I really looked forward to doing it again; I wanted that shit in me. Like a lot of drunks report, introducing alcohol into my body just felt like, *"Ooh, there we go. Here I am."* Sort of like it elegantly completed a chemical equation of some kind.

But I never really had a honeymoon period with alcohol. Even an idiot or a kitten observing my first drunken experience would describe it as awful. Still, I sought booze with a fervor measurably more intense than that with which I sought to get into young women's underpants, which is to say it made Hercules (or Jason Statham) look like a pussy.

The summer before my sophomore year of high school, I drank a bottle of tequila at a friend's house. Someone handed me a joint and I took a hit, and immediately a wave of nausea hit me. I knew I was going to puke so I covered my mouth with my hand. All this did was intensify the pressure, and when the puke freed itself, it did so in the form of a powerful vomit laser that escaped from between my fingers and hit a guy in the face.

That night, my friend Todd took me home from the party and we sat on my front porch smoking cigarettes. It was probably around nine or ten and my mom was out with a friend. After a bit, I got up and walked across the street to a telephone pole. Unlike most telephone poles, this one had handles hammered into it that allowed one to reach up and climb it with relative ease if you were over six feet tall. I jumped up and grabbed the first handles and began to climb. It didn't take long to get to the top. I relaxed and surveyed the neighborhood. Everything looked good. We lived on Ruby Avenue in a neighborhood that also included the Avenues Emerald and Sapphire.

I had delivered the *Boston Globe* for several years as a younger kid and as a result, I'd been inside at least fifty of the houses I could see from my perch.

After some addled thought, I reached out to the telephone wires. (I'm assuming they were telephone wires and not electrical wires, since I'm typing this as an alive, non-crispy person.) I then hung my full weight from the wires and began to "walk" with my hands, out and away from the telephone pole and twenty-five or so feet above the street.

Todd watched my progress from the ground. My "plan" was to try to make it to the next telephone pole. The task grew difficult pretty quickly however, and I became too tired to make it. At that point, I couldn't make it back to the telephone pole I'd started from either. So I let go of the wire. I fell, rather far, to the street below and my feet hit the ground maybe a tenth of a second before my forehead did. I remained conscious but began to bleed from a new hole I'd made above my left eyebrow. Todd's mouth was frozen in an "O" shape from the shock of seeing it all. It took him a while to relax.

We went back to my front steps and smoked some more cigarettes until my mom got home and took me to the hospital to get sewed up. For many years she believed that I had tripped over our cat, Lava. Because that's what I told her had happened. I figured it was better for her sanity to believe that her son was a drunk klutz than an actively suicidal daredevil with the stunt proficiency of a trash bag filled with blueberry yogurt.

When my sophomore year began, I was suspended for coming to school hung over. My chemistry teacher said I was acting weird, so I was brought to the vice principal's office where I was given a breathalyzer test. I don't know what I blew, but it was more than zero, so I was suspended for a week. My mom seemed to divide her anger, focusing twenty-five percent of it at me and the other seventy-five percent of it at the vice principal. How dare they punish me based on a measurement system approved by law enforcement officials across the world! She felt vindicated when I took a breathalyzer to get readmitted to school and the mouthwash I'd used that morning registered as .001 or so on the machine. I then rinsed my mouth out in the vice principal's bathroom sink and blew a zero, allowing my mom to continue to hold a grudge against Ms. Loomis, Marblehead High School's vice principal in 1992. Not that my mom wouldn't (and didn't) punish me; she just was one of those parents who preferred to do it "in-house," and seeing any other adult exert any authority over her own kid pissed her off whether it made sense or not.

That same year, my friend Michael had a party and we got an older guy who had U2 vanity plates on his car to buy us booze. While all my friends had him get them a six-pack of beer, I got a bottle of Jack Daniel's. I got drunk quickly and blacked out early in the evening. I'm told I stripped naked and went into Michael's younger sister's closet (she wasn't home) and put on her Halloween costume, which was a cheap polyester skeleton costume. I was already six foot three and the costume was made for a child. It was terribly tight and looked like a unitard for murderers. My dick and balls bulged through the diaphanous material. Though it was technically a Halloween costume, I'm sure its designers never imagined it would be worn in such a terrifying scenario. I then went up the stairs back to the party.

At the time, my friends Michael, Pat, Chad, and I had a band called "Scaramanga." Francisco Scaramanga was the name of the villain in the James Bond film *The Man with the Golden Gun.* In the beginning of the film, Bond finds out that while no one in British Intelligence has seen Scaramanga's face, he does have the distinguishing characteristic of having a prominent third nipple. So Bond poses as Scaramanga, wearing a prosthetic third nipple.

I remember Michael looking through a Bond encyclopedia for band name ideas and when he brought to my attention the fact that there was a man in whose honor a prosthetic third nipple had been designed and worn, I said, "That's our band name." And so it was.

The night of Michael's party we'd set up our equipment to play some Huey Lewis songs to entertain our friends. I was immediately too drunk, but when I reemerged from downstairs as a hulking girl-skeleton with a beefy cockpouch, I sat on a couch and screamed unintelligibly into a microphone for a few minutes anyway. Then I got up, walked back to the top of the stairs, and leapt down the whole flight. At the bottom, my head went through a very nice stained glass window. Miraculously, my head popped out several pieces of the window from the lead outlines that held it together and no glass actually shattered.

I've offered the above anecdotes because they highlight that I had bad, potentially fatal things happen as a result of my drinking right out of the gate. And I kept on drinking. Through high school, through college, and then for a few more years after that, while the blackouts, pissed beds and couches, and sickness continued to pile up. I won't catalog every event, as a laundry list would get tiring to read pretty quickly. Suffice to say that alcohol and I never mixed well.

I went to college at New York University. While there were hundreds of excellent schools in the great city of Boston, I wanted to live in the biggest city of all, plus NYU was the destination for kids who wanted to do musical theater *with their lives*, which is what I fantasized about when I was seventeen. I didn't really have the grades to get into NYU my freshman through junior year of high school, so for my senior year I buckled down and got straight A's. This, shockingly, was easier than putting myself through the mental and emotional contortions of procrastination that netted me C's for the first three years of high school. My SATs were good, since I'd pretty much jerked off to standardized tests ever since the first one I took in elementary school. Fill in a dot and get a prize? Yes, please. In the ambiguity and shifting playing field of adult life, I often wish I could just fill in a dot and have someone say "Yes" and hand me a chicken leg, or "No" and slap me with an old fish. I got accepted based on my grades and test scores, but also based on the monologue and two songs I performed for a man in a tiny studio who wouldn't let me shake his hand when I was done because he said he'd recently blown his nose into it.

Wisely, whoever ran the housing department at NYU decided to provide mattresses that were covered in sturdy plastic. After running a large university for over a century, the university's data must have determined that students were pissing themselves frequently enough to justify an all-plastic mattress policy. And piss myself on their mattresses I did! And not just my own. At the end of my freshman year I fell asleep on my roommate Rohit's bed when he was out of town. I'd taken a girl to a screening of *The Umbrellas of Cherbourg* and I'd struck out. So I convinced my other roommates to drink ten or fifteen beers with me, then passed out in Rohit's bed instead of my own and pissed in it very thoroughly. When I woke up and realized what had happened, I sprang into action. I washed his comforter, sheets, and mattress pad. Then I dried them and, in the process, melted his mattress pad. Great holes were seared into it, all over, but I put it on his bed anyway with the sheets and comforter over it. When he got back to the dorms, lay down on his bed, and felt the crunchy mattress pad under him, he pulled the sheets off and asked the Heavens, "What the fuck?"

Rather than admit I'd passed out on his bed and irrigated it, I told him, "Sometimes mattress pads melt under your sheets when it gets hot." I don't know if he believed this, but we didn't speak of it again, and we went to our respective homes for the summer a few days later. He is a vice president at Citibank now, as is another of our suitemates, Guang, with whom I smoked pot regularly through a hose that hooked up to a Vietnam-era gas mask that we would take turns strapping to our faces.

I graduated in 1999 and moved in with my friend Kiyash

into an apartment in Alphabet City—a charming area of downtown New York. The main differences between then and now were that very few people had cell phones and I thought it was okay to wear tank tops. One rainy night, soon after moving in with Kiyash, I called 911 because there was a man with no legs who had fallen out of his wheelchair, drunk, and passed out in the gutter. When the EMTs responded I helped them lift the drunk into the ambulance. Life can be a real cunt sometimes.

The best thing about that apartment was its view of the Empire State Building. I used to sit inside and watch it get struck by lightning during storms. That's a question I'd ask Accountant-Zeus: How many bolts of lightning did you hurl at that motherfucker? I saw it happen at least fifty times in one year. It's a real spiritual palate cleanser too; I hope you get to see the Empire State Building get struck by lightning sometime in your life. It's much more exciting than riding a fart-filled elevator up to the top and having the powerful wind blow your Cardinals hat off your head. You can't think about anything else when you're watching a tall building get struck by lightning, either. Ayn Rand and Howard Roark can take turns sucking my dick while Sarah Palin takes pictures, but a skyscraper is a magical thing and watching nature turn one into a hundred-story lightning rod is like watching heaven and earth bumpin' pretties.

At the Alphabet City apartment, I slept on a futon, which was not coated in plastic. As such, the fact that I pissed aggressively into it every few nights surely tripled its weight over time. I know because, when I eventually moved out, I could barely carry it down the four flights of stairs to throw it on the

Alphabet City sidewalk for a sanitation worker or homeless person to deal with.

Over the next two years, I drank a lot. I rarely drank every day, since whenever I started there was no real way to tell if I'd go totally off the rails and black out or pass out somewhere. I acted in musicals, plays, and had the odd small role on *All My Children*. Susan Lucci was very nice. Josh Duhamel was very muscular. I also happened to be an extra on one episode of *Saturday Night Live* in a fake commercial for a reality show called *The Cannibal*, where you had to figure out if the cannibal was me or Will Ferrell. It was Will Ferrell. I remember him eating pieces of real ham covered in fake blood and being understandably grossed out by it.

My girlfriend at the time was bummed out by my drinking, but not horrified. She never really saw it all, since I'd try to keep it together around her. One time I yelled at her in the street when she tried to get me to come home with her after a lovely date where we'd had a few drinks, rather than go to a bar where I said I had friends "waiting for me." There were no friends there; I'd lied, and then went there and drank alone until I was garbage. I brought her flowers the next day and I very clearly remember her roommate glaring at me with the wholly warranted disgust you focus on a textbook scumbag. Beyond that, I'd try to sound chipper when I spoke to my mom on the phone and mask the depression in my voice that attended my hangovers. I was basically "trucking along" as a functional drunk who knew he had a problem but hoped nothing truly terrible would happen. I'd quit for weeks or months at a time, which allowed me to feel physically much better and not piss in my bed, but I'd always start again, picking up—AS A RULE—right where I'd left off.

In 2001, two years after graduating, during which I'd lived with Kiyash, toured the U.S. as Sir Lancelot in a national tour of the musical *Camelot*, and worked as a bellboy at the Hudson Hotel, I moved from New York to L.A.

I had decided to finally buy a real bed after having destroyed my final New York futon and throwing it on the sidewalk in Queens as my neighbor's big fuzzy Akita cheerily barked "What are you doing?" at me. I loved that dog. I never got to hug and roll around with him (or her; fuck if I can tell what a dog's gender is if it doesn't clearly display its junk to me) the way we would've liked, but I spent hours petting him over a fence and talking to him.

After arriving in L.A. and securing an apartment in Silver-lake, I dialed 1-800-MATTRESS and ordered a queen-size bed. It was a big step—deciding to stop peeing in a futon and start peeing in a real bed—and I took it seriously. When I went to Bed Bath &Beyond to buy sheets along with a little trash can and a bathmat and such, I knew I'd also need plastic sheets for my queen-size bed. I was a big boy now, and big boys pee in big beds! I walked right up to a young woman in her blue Bed Bath & Beyond apron and asked her where the plastic sheets were. She told me they were in the kids' linen section with other kids' things.

"Uh, I'm looking for plastic sheets for a *queen-size* bed."

"Oh . . ."

"Yep."

"Oh, um, we don't have those. We could order them?"

"Well, then, yeah. Order them."

In a moment of utter sobriety, I was one hundred percent at peace with the fact that I was a voluntary, habitual, adult bedwetter and I was comfortable discussing it frankly with a stranger.

Yes, there were flashier episodes in my drinking career, like car crashes and drunken fights with my girlfriend in the middle of the street, but the elegance of asking a stranger to help me find a specialty product that helped me reduce the damage that my routine bedwetting caused was a beautiful, shimmering red flag.

la peur

My dad and I watched *One Flew Over the Cuckoo's Nest* when I was maybe ten or so and it blew my young mind. It's the first film I can remember that made me weep. Interestingly, my parents' first date was going to see the theatrical production of *Cuckoo's Nest* when it was staged in Boston. Hell of a first date, guys. It should also be noted that a pigeon shit on my dad's head as they walked through Boston Common on their way to the theater. I may as well also tell you that on a recent morning I was walking with my son in his little carrier on my chest and a bird shit so copiously that it got on both my son and me. So that is three living generations of Delaney men who have functioned as toilets for birds. May the tradition continue! I'm not aware of any stories of my grandfather Bill being shit on, although my dad did tell me that as a kid during the Depression he and his friends would pick horse shit up off the ground and throw it at one another for fun. That is all I know about Delaney men and animal shit. If you know anything I don't, please contact my publisher.

One Flew Over the Cuckoo's Nest was on TV another time when I was young. My parents were out and our beloved babysitter Lauren was watching us. Lauren said she didn't want me to watch it because I would cry and she didn't want to deal with that. I promised her I wouldn't cry and begged her to let me watch it. But when our hero, the beautiful, elemental McMurphy, was lobotomized after attacking the cuntly Nurse Ratched, CRY I DID. I sobbed. And so did Lauren! I think, having seen it before too, she knew that *she* would cry and she didn't want to deal with *that*.

It's actually a treasured memory of mine; both of us crying, Lauren saying between sobs, "I told you I didn't want you to watch it! I told you you'd cry!" I laugh to think about it.

Lauren was a very good babysitter who watched my sister Maggie and me for years. As an adult and now a parent, I recognize the importance of carefully choosing the people you leave with your kids. Lauren sort of felt like a third parent or an older sister to me. I thought she was the coolest thing that ever happened. Her favorite band was Duran Duran. Thus, my favorite band was Duran Duran. When her mercurial teenage tastes changed overnight, and Tears for Fears became her favorite band, I immediately followed suit, removing all the pictures of Duran Duran's keyboard player Nick Rhodes from my bedroom wall and replacing them with pictures of Tears for Fears's Curt Smith. Since my adolescence and the last years of my parents' marriage coincided, Lauren felt like a safe person to be around and admire. I could complain to her and just be an eleven-year-old. I remain grateful that she was the babysitter my parents chose to hire.

When I was a freshman in high school I saw Martin Scorsese's remake of *Cape Fear*. I also saw and read Thomas Harris's *The Silence of the Lambs* and *Red Dragon* that year. It was a time in my life when I enjoyed being terrified. My parents were getting divorced and I think it was somehow comforting to watch actual madmen hurt people terribly. On some level I thought, *Well, at least* that's *not happening in my home.* I'd always loved reading and fantasizing but when my life became painful on a day-to-day basis, escaping into books, movies, and music became necessary in addition to "fun." I also began to drink more frequently around that time, and I thought about drinking constantly. I don't pin my drinking on my parents' divorce. I drank when I was sad or when I was happy, and so many members of my family are alcoholics or in recovery that I'm pretty sure alcoholism was in the cards for me, whether my parents divorced or not. Alcohol allowed me to toy with fear, map its edges, and try to exercise a little control over it. The operative word being "try," since I would routinely be ejected from the driver's seat of my body and mind when I got drunk. My drinking got worse throughout high school and into college, and while it wasn't always dramatic, it would be punctuated every few months or so by events genuinely dangerous or, at best, frightening.

One Easter weekend when I was home from NYU, I went with my mom and my uncle Johnny to pick up a honeyed ham for our big family meal. The honeyed ham place was out on the old Route 1 in Danvers, Massachusetts. Danvers, it is fascinating to note, was not always called Danvers. Three hundred years ago it was known as Salem Village. Growing up I'd assumed the events leading to the Salem Witch Trials of 1692 took place in plain old Salem, which still very much exists. But at some point along the way, Salem Village changed its name to Danvers. While the actual witch trials took place in what's now downtown Salem, the events that led up to them took place in Danvers. So whether or not you believe in any type of "Other," be it good, bad, or something beyond either, there is a strong argument to be made that Danvers is charged with some intense metaphysical juju.

My travels rarely took me out that way but whenever they did, the black iron spires of Danvers State Hospital looming over the treetops in the distance called to me. At that time in my life, my dreams were often about architecture and civil engineering. Most nights I traveled through factories and warehouses and armories, just exploring. I hung out in sewers and air ducts and subway systems. It was wonderful. Something about man-made passageways and storage areas and transportation systems just excites me, and always has. I'll practically jerk off to photographs of abandoned and dilapidated buildings. And old mental institutions? Don't get me started.

Heaven, for me, would be a place with unfettered access to old, shut-down hospitals and the ruins of train stations. Seeing these massive, useful, beautiful structures and systems rot and fall apart reminds me that even things made of iron and stone will collapse and be swallowed up by the earth, which will in turn be eaten by the sun. That doesn't depress me at all; rather, I find it invigorating. So I mentioned to my mom and uncle that I'd always wanted to check out Danvers Hospital.

The hospital had closed some years before and was falling apart by this time, but my uncle Johnny was on the Danvers Board of Historical Preservation, so he thought he could probably get us in there for a tour. He added that there were developers who were very interested in tearing down the hospital and turning it into condos or stores and that its days were likely numbered. He suggested we just drive up as close as we could and check it out. And so we did.

I'd heard scary stories about the hospital over the years; one childhood neighbor of my mother's had been committed there. And my friend had told me this horrifying story: He knew a receptionist at the hospital who operated a switchboard. One day someone forgot to lock a door behind her and a female patient, who was both insane and the size of a linebacker, opened the door, grabbed the receptionist's head, and smashed it into the switchboard, breaking most of the bones in her face.

Historically Danvers State Hospital was also famous for the number of lobotomies it gave. In the early part of the twentieth century, doctors would give lobotomies to people for the tiniest reasons, like depression or having a "bad temper." Not that there ever is a *good* reason to stick a scalpel behind someone's eyeball and swirl it around. If there isn't something in the Hippocratic Oath that directly forbids using a "swirling" action with a scalpel, there should be. Is there a lazier motion? Swerving? Fiddling? One famous Massachusetts lobotomy of the early twentieth century was the one Joseph Kennedy ordered up for his daughter Rosemary when she was twenty-three years old. She'd suffered from mood swings, so he had her lobotomized without even consulting his wife. It makes me cry to think about these people, especially when I've been the beneficiary of such wonderful modern psychiatric care. We can and should complain about certain horrors of the modern world, but when it comes to the treatment of mental illness, the advances made in the last hundred years have been far more significant than the space program, nuclear fission, or even *The Wire*, for so many fortunate people.

Danvers State Hospital also had a field of unmarked graves where patients who died and were left unclaimed were buried. I like to imagine that those dead, unloved nutjobs became friends under the earth and have a little crazy corpse community where they show one another the kindnesses they were denied while living.

My mother, uncle, and I exited off the highway and drove through some beautiful New England farmland studded with huge old maple trees that were covered in bright green April leaves, each one big enough to cover your privates in a sixteenth-century-style Christian painting. We headed toward the looming black spires and passed a still-active residential psychiatric facility for kids. We began to climb the hill that leads to Danvers State itself but had to stop at a locked gate that closed off the road. We pulled over and parked. Uncle Johnny thought it was a good idea to continue on foot and my mom and I, for some reason, agreed.

I should mention that Johnny is insane and had he been born a century or even seventy-five years earlier, it would not be difficult to imagine him as a resident of the hospital we were now approaching on foot. He's a loud, flamboyant man who will break out into song in a powerful bass voice for no reason at all. He owns an insurance agency in Beverly, Massachusetts, and has a massive old house to which he'll occasionally add a new wing as the mood strikes him. The great room in the center of his house is co-commanded by a grand, ornate chandelier he bought on a whim in Argentina and an extended Steinway concert grand piano. Just so we're clear: This piano is larger than a grand piano. Did you know there was a piano bigger than a grand piano? Well, there is, and he plays it beautifully. He's also active in community theater; he once shaved his head to play Daddy Warbucks, and he actually painted himself dark brown to play one of the Wise Men in *Amahl and the Night Visitors*. A few years ago, he also decided that he was a painter and almost immediately began producing shockingly good landscapes. He just doesn't do things halfway.

That's why Johnny was, not surprisingly, the leader of this field trip. That my mother was a part of it is beyond bananas.

While she's funny and fun to be around and very curious intellectually, she is the OPPOSITE of physically adventurous. She might happily read and discuss an article about a family trespassing on the grounds of an abandoned mental hospital, but I would have bet all my paper-route money that she would have told you to fuck off if you invited her to actually join such an endeavor. But join it she did.

As I said, we surveyed the road ahead and the hill that rose up on our left, leading to the hospital. It was obvious that it would save time if we left the road, got out of the car, and just climbed up the hill. In fairy tales, we're told it's a bad idea to leave the path. That's because it's often a bad idea in real life. This was one of those times. Immediately upon leaving the path, the ground was *weird*. It looked like a normal grass-covered hill, but the ground yielded in an odd way under our feet. Instead of walking up the hill, we were scrambling. I fell at least once.

I joked to my mom, "Even the ground seems haunted."

She forced a weak smile as if to say, *I'm not terrified!*

We continued our climb for fifty yards or so and then crested the hill, broke through the strip of trees, and beheld the formidable Danvers State Hospital in its full majesty. It was glorious. Seen from the air in photographs, it looks like a mighty bat, or perhaps a flock of carnivorous geese, flying silently in a soulless black V through the stratosphere. There is the central heart and head of the building and then it spans out and back to each side in receding wings. For sheer internal volume the only non-skyscraper building that could compare would be a major city's National Guard armory. It was massive. It was bigger than your urban high school plus your first apartment building plus the theater you saw your first concert in. It was FUCKING HUGE. And until recently it had been packed full of people who needed to be encouraged daily that they weren't, for example, Henry VIII, or that they shouldn't insist that everyone on the trolley sniff their genitals. There were a few other buildings on the grounds—staff residences and a church. But they were all dwarfed, or perhaps shamed, by the main hospital building's utter magnificence.

We approached the main building silently, the way you would approach a cathedral or a butte in Arizona at sunset. It was four stories tall and made of red brick. It had a slate roof, just like my elementary school. My fourth-grade science teacher once held up a piece of slate that had fallen off the school roof and said, "This could have cut your head off." Never, not ever again in my life, have I seen a slate roof without imagining a slate coming loose, skittering down the incline, gaining speed, jumping over the gutter, and then sailing a few stories through the air before it neatly decapitated me. IT IS SO CURIOUS how hearing something once in your youth can dictate a thought pattern all the way through your life. I was nine, a man said something nonchalantly, and now when I see slate at age thirty-six, as far as I'm concerned, its primary use is for beheading boys. Once that's done, it can be used for roofing.

We stood reverently and took in the building. All the windows on the first story were boarded up with plywood that had been painted the same shade of red as the building's bricks. The windows on the second, third, and fourth floors were caged. A school desk with an attached chair had been thrown through a window on the fourth floor, smashing it, but the cage had effectively "caught" it, so the chair teetered, swaying back and forth in the wind, using part of the window's surviving frame as a fulcrum and occasionally banging loudly into the cage. If you were directing a horror film and the art director had placed the eerie old school desk in the window's frame so that any breeze would bang it menacingly into the mental hospital's anti-escape and -suicide cage windows, you'd say, "Okay, Terry, that's a bit much. We don't want to go overboard on the creepiness right away . . . ." I mean, I want to believe that some idiot vandal broke in and did it, but it's also possible that it was the only reminder of a frustrated and terrified seventeen-year-old's final attempt to escape a pair of burly orderlies who'd been sent to spirit him to the basement lobotomy lair. My mom and uncle and I looked up at the desk and then at one another. It was as good of a "You Should Not Be Here" red flag as I'll probably ever see, but we ignored it totally.

We milled around the outside, exploring all the while, making sure no cops or security guards were about or, worse yet, former inmates who'd gone feral and occasionally snuck back out of the woods to grab and eat trespassers.

The main entrance was barred, boarded, and impenetrable, but after a bit of casual exploration I found an auxiliary door at ground level. Where its padlock should have been, there was a twig. I removed the twig and cracked the door. Though I was twenty, I ran back to my mom and uncle like a four-year-old and said, "Look, Mom! Look what I found! An open door! Do you wanna go in?" I should add that I asked them if they wanted to go in because I felt that it was my duty as an allegedly adventurous young man to do so. I hoped, however, that they would say, "Fuck, no. Are you crazy?" I really, really only wanted the right to say, after the fact, that I'd asked them to go in but, old farty wet noodles that they were, they said no. BUT THEY SAID YES! My insurance agent mom and insurance agent uncle, who should have done a speedy risk analysis and assessed the likelihood of us getting kidnapped and turned into human beef jerky, said yes! So I had to say, "Okay, terrific, because I really wanted to go in too!"

We marched quietly to the door and entered Danvers State Hospital. The doorway opened onto a hallway at the base of a staircase, which, like the windows on the outside of the building, was caged. I hadn't seen a caged staircase before, and for those who haven't, it's disturbing. You can walk up and down it, like any old staircase, but if you wanted to jump over the railing at any point or jump between the flights as the stairs go from floor to floor, you can't. Right away, Danvers State announces itself as a place with a strong "No suicides, please" policy. Commendable, I think.

The paint had peeled off the walls in sheets and flakes. It decorated the floor in ugly constellations. The afternoon light came in shafts through any windows that weren't boarded over, so we were able to see reasonably well. Opposite the bottom of the staircase was an open door from which you could see the top of another smaller staircase, leading underground. I approached the door but gazing into the basement of the dilapidated mental hospital that I'd broken into with my mom—where hundreds of lobotomies were performed and where, if you died, you might literally be thrown into an unmarked ditch out back—induced paralyzing fear in me. The BEST-case scenario was that not less than ten thousand rats lived down there in the darkness and had birthday bowling parties with the skulls of former patients. The basement was dark, but not dark in the sense that it was "not light." It was so dark that it gave the impression we were under crystal-clear water and the basement was filled with squid ink that stopped right at the door frame, held in place by an invisible membrane that appeared to pulse against the light. I have never seen a blacker black, even with my eyes closed at night in the cedar closet of my childhood home where I would sometimes hide among the raincoats, old costumes, and my dad's uniforms and fatigues from Vietnam. This was a dark that knew things. I'm sure it would have loved to envelop us and tell us its stories, but I was one hundred percent certain I didn't want to hear any of them. I backed away from the darkness of the hospital basement's mouth and rejoined my mom and Johnny.

The caged staircase seemed to draw us toward it. We slowly, nervously climbed to the next floor, all the while secure in the knowledge that the caging surrounding us would thwart any spontaneous suicidal urges. We reached the second floor and rounded a corner, revealing a long hallway lined on both sides with cell-like rooms. The hallway was bare; there was very little garbage or extra furniture or just general detritus one might expect to find in a condemned hospital that had stood for well over a century. My guess is that anything the state hadn't taken away to other, still functioning hospitals or thrown away had been taken by scavengers or trespassers like us. If my mom had any hopes of getting her hands on a vintage trepanning drill, she was out of luck that day.

We stuck close together, because fuck you if I was going to get separated from my mommy in that place. Moms are comforting and moms are safe. Even as an adult, if I really, really go deep in my psyche to search for the "safest" feeling I can, it remains me as a four-year-old, resting my head in my mom's lap as she cleaned my ears with a Q-tip. We poked our heads into one of the residential rooms that lined the hallway. It was empty, in the sense that there was no furniture or any physical items in the room. But it didn't feel empty. It felt full, the way you feel deep underwater when your ears need to pop. Although the room was as modestly sized as a college dorm room, the ceiling was absurdly high. Not only could you not touch the ceiling if you jumped up in the air, an NBA center couldn't have touched it. Really the only place a ceiling should be that high is in a ballroom or a cathedral. All three of us agreed that the oddly high ceilings made the room feel like a horrible tube at the bottom of which any resident would just be waiting for a giant hand to tear the roof off, reach down to root around the room, grab its inmate, and toss him or her into its maw. My feeling was that if you were not crazy when they put you in this room, you would become crazy pretty quickly as your mind's contents unspooled and were drawn up toward the roof in the cyclonic weather pattern the room's design encouraged.

We exited the room and continued down the hall. More rooms lined the hall, like a terrible hotel. We declined to look into any others. At the end of the hall was a large and open room that looked like a locker-room shower and changing area, except that all the fixtures had been removed, so it was just a lot of white tiles and porcelain, with bathtub- and sink-shaped holes here and there. It reminded me of the famous bathroom area in *One Flew Over the Cuckoo's Nest* where wild man Randle P. McMurphy tries to tear the hydrotherapy console out of the floor and throw it through the window to escape from the mental hospital where he was a guest. There was a hole in the floor we were walking on that was reminiscent of the one produced by McMurphy's friend, the Chief, when he finally succeeded in tearing out the console and breaking out.

After milling around the shower facility, imagining patients being hosed off en masse, my mom, Johnny, and I decided to make our way on out into the sunlight and hit the road. We had an Easter ham to deliver, after all.

On our way out I spotted a booklet on the ground against a wall. It was dusty and had acquired the color of its surroundings, though when my fingers' oils had lifted away some of the gray it appeared to have once been green. I picked it up and leafed through it and I am so very glad I did. It was a guide on how to convert the hospital into an emergency safe house that could shelter thousands of people from the surrounding communities alongside its normal insane residents IN THE EVENT OF A NUCLEAR WAR. It was from the 1960s, when people were genuinely concerned about the possibility of global nuclear holocaust, but still, come on, man! Can you (even if given twenty minutes and a cool, quiet place to think with no distractions) POSSIBLY think of a more bananas scenario? A functioning, fully occupied gothic mental hospital that had witnessed countless human lifetimes of horror, throwing open its doors to offer shelter to the "normal" people from nearby towns during a nuclear fucking war? No! No, you cannot come up with something crazier. I mean, maybe, if Auschwitz had opened its doors to house local Polish families in the event of a global zombie outbreak? But this Danvers Crazies 'n' Normies Side by Side in Nuclear Harmony COULD have happened! And clearly a consulting firm sat around and wrote a fucking guide book about it that had survived a few decades and sat there for me to find! Of course I put it in my back pocket and took it home to study.

Somewhat surprisingly, this was the thing that finally upset and frightened my mom. She felt that a physical item from the hospital would have ghosts or evil spirits attached to it, and that they would roam our home at night and crawl inside our heads and make us crazy. And that's not a joke; she would always say when we were younger that she wasn't afraid of things like *Jaws*, because if you could just get to shore, your problems would be over. But things like *The Exorcist* could get into your head and control you and how the fuck were you supposed to combat that? To be fair, I was nervous about having the book in our home too, so that night I put it in our back hall closet by our boots and coats and umbrellas. Come morning it was gone. My mom had thrown it away. So I remain unschooled in the ways of converting a mental hospital into a bomb shelter.

To date, that remains the last time my mom and I broke into a mental institution, abandoned or otherwise. If you haven't done it yourself, you really must. We got to experience fascinating history laced with genuine terror on that spring afternoon in Danvers. And unlike most people who'd spent any time there, we were allowed to leave.

Not long after, the hospital was razed and replaced with bland condominiums, whose residents surely share their beds with lobotomized ghosts who sing them to sleep with the saddest lullabies in the world.

la mer

For two summers during college, 1997 and 1998, I quit New York for Marblehead and drove a boat called a "launch" on Marblehead Harbor. A launch is a glorified water taxi that takes rich people out to the middle of the harbor, where their boats are moored. Marblehead, a town of twenty thousand souls, has five yacht clubs. I'd be very surprised if there were another town on our planet that had a higher number of yacht clubs per capita. The Eastern, Boston, Dolphin, and Marblehead Yacht Clubs had their own launch services. The Crescent Yacht Club employed me and I drove its members, exclusively, from the dock to their various opulent sailboats and powerboats.

Our busiest day and night of the summer was always the Fourth of July. A wealthy community, Marblehead could afford to mount a high-quality fireworks display. Also, since Marblehead is a peninsula with a large island that's attached by a thin causeway, its natural harbor is both protected from the open sea and surrounded by land on three sides. So, the harbor is several square miles of water filled with around two thousand boats, ringed by beaches and docks and parks. You'd be hard pressed to find a better place to drink fourteen beers and watch fireworks. Though my earliest Fourth of Julys found me sitting on my dad's shoulders and watching fireworks from the beach, after puberty I saw the holiday as one of the few days of the year when it was perfectly acceptable to drink into unconsciousness.

The launch would operate nonstop on the Fourth, ferrying people to and from their boats. Then, after the fireworks, my fellow launch operators and I would respond to radio calls and pick up families with kids, old couples, and dangerously crowded motorboats filled with drunk people in their twenties. Our staff consisted of our boss—Dockmaster Bill; my high school friend and bandmate—Michael; a couple other college kids; and me. Bill was a salty dog in his forties who'd grown up on the water and worked at the Crescent for at least ten years. Michael and I had known each other since we were about seven and then became very close in high school when we were both heavily involved in theater, as well as drinking and talking about boobs.

Our workday finished up at eleven p.m. and then we were

free to get into whatever trouble we felt like getting into. For Michael and me, in the summer of 1998, that meant getting drunk, appropriating a little dinghy that belonged to the yacht club, and using it to cruise around the harbor to see who was out and about. It wasn't rare for us to take the twelve-foot motorboat out for a drunken cruise in the middle of the night. We'd do this a few times every summer with no real fear of getting in trouble, since drunken shenanigans on the high seas of Massachusetts are as run-of-the-mill as mustaches on cops.

Being filled with beer and on the water is something people have been doing since they figured out how to ferment hops, and it's easy to understand why. It's fun and it feels good. You've thinned your blood with the alcohol that's sloshing around in your belly, complementing the rise and fall of the sea you're floating upon. It just feels right to have booze in your guts as you float around Mother Ocean, like a dumb, fat buoy, at the mercy of the sea and filled with spirits. Sailors refer to the ocean as "the drink" too, as in "I slipped and grabbed for a halyard, and my wrench fell in the drink," so clearly there's something substantial and enduring to this alcohol/sea connection.

Sometimes Michael and I would putt out to Children's Island—an island about a mile beyond the mouth of the harbor—and go for a stroll. Growing up, I'd gone to day camp on Children's Island for years, and it felt entirely naughty to trespass on it as a drunken adult. Like most islands around New England, it smelled like seagull shit and wild grass. I'm sure if I caught a whiff of it right now I'd start crying.

When I was a counselor on the island, I'd had to become a

certified lifeguard. Part of the training consisted of an overnight springtime visit to the island where we were supposed to
practice different rescue techniques. Upon arrival, we discovered that the Marblehead cop who taught the course was insane. He must have been certified forty years ago over the
telephone or something. Clearly no one was checking up on
him, because he had gone entirely "rogue" and used educational techniques that were, I now realize, abusive. The most
memorable thing he did was show us a slideshow of ACTUAL
DEAD DROWNING VICTIMS from Marblehead police
files.

He began the slideshow by asking, "What's the difference
between a saltwater drowning and a freshwater drowning? . . .
I'll tell you: saltwater animals eat people, freshwater animals
don't. So when you find someone who's drowned in saltwater,
they'll have been eaten somewhat, and when you find someone
who's drowned in freshwater, they'll be all bloated up. So what
you find is horrible, just in two different ways."

He then got out a slide projector, positioned it in front of a
white sheet that was suspended in front of a fireplace, and
started showing us pictures of a variety of corpses that had been
pulled out of the water a few miles in various directions from
where we sat in our sleeping bags, in a lodge, on a small island,
in the middle of the dark terrifying night. My friend Ellen was
there; we were adhered to each other in fear as he clicked from
corpse to corpse. The island didn't have electricity, so the slide
projector was powered by a portable gas generator that
hummed outside of the building, efficiently masking the sounds

of any approaching ghosts or child murderers. One particularly ghastly saltwater drowning victim was a skeleton whose meat had been almost entirely removed from it. Almost. The gut contents within the rib cage had proven difficult to access for the fish and bottom feeders, so the ribs rather effectively "caged" a rotten buffet of guts that poked out the bottom and protruded between the ribs. The slide that followed that was of a dead baby. A fucking dead baby! And since this baby had drowned in freshwater, it was bloated and huge. Next photo was a close-up of the dead baby's bloated face. We cringed and then the screen immediately went black and the generator went out. Then it came back on. Then off again. The generator sputtered. The dead baby's face strobed on and off as the generator outside choked and a room full of sixteen-year-olds screamed. WHAT IN CHRIST'S FUCK DID THIS HAVE TO DO WITH LIFEGUARDING!!!! Twenty years later, my best guess remains *"Not a thing."* Officer Soulmurder went out to check on the generator, and when he returned he said, "Bad news; the generator broke." We shuddered in relief and then went outside to practice moving people with spine injuries from one end of the island to another.

Sadly, that next summer, a man named Thomas Maimoni took a woman he'd just met named Martha Brailsford out for a sail, killed her, and threw her body in the ocean behind Children's Island. When she first disappeared, Maimoni said he didn't know what had happened; they'd finished their sail and upon getting back to land he hadn't seen her again. But, some days later a lobsterman was pulling up his traps, and up came

Martha on his line. I, thank goodness, was on the other side of the island teaching a small boatload of ten-year-olds how to sail. But my friend Doug so happened to witness her being moved from the lobster boat to the police boat, and he was able to confirm that saltwater fish do, in fact, like to snack on people.

But on the Fourth of July, as our shift ended, Michael and I were in a very jovial mood. We cracked open our cooler of beers and downed a few, getting drunk very quickly. We then motored around and said hello to people, drinking beer and smoking cigarettes. While I rarely smoked when I wasn't drinking, I chain-smoked when I drank, and it wasn't rare for me to go through two packs in a night.

As we circumnavigated the harbor, one particularly loud powerboat caught our attention. It was about a twenty-five-foot cabin cruiser. We pulled up next to it and started talking to its passengers in that easy manner that drunks around the world have: "Hey, you're drunk, I'm drunk, let's be best friends immediately!" A group of two guys and two girls in their thirties were onboard. Neither Michael nor I had ever met any of them before, but we chatted for a bit, and then we invited them onto our boat to cruise around. They got off their very nice boat and onto our twelve-foot open dinghy. Six full-grown adults were forced to jockey for comfort on the tiniest vessel on the sea worthy of the label "boat." Weighed down considerably, we headed for the mouth of the harbor.

A famous three-hulled sailboat or trimaran called the *Great American II* was moored at the mouth of the harbor. The *Great American II* was famous because it had broken the record

65

for circumnavigating the globe that was set by a guy named Magellan. How amazing is that? *The Guinness Book of World Records* is filled with things like "Most Consecutive Weeks at Number One on the Billboard Charts" or "Largest Goiter." The motherfuckers on the *Great American II* sailed around the planet faster than fucking Magellan. That really makes all other record setters look like small potatoes. Micro-potatoes. Potatettes. What's that? Can you not see it? No, you can't; it's ants laughing at tiny little potatettes through their ant-microscope. Don't use a magnifying glass to look at them or they will ignite. Sorry to go on; I just want to drive home the magnificence of a crew that sails around the world so fast it causes a record from five hundred years ago, set by a bad-ass son of a bitch, to go up in flames.

One thing that Michael and I liked to do was build up some speed in the dinghy and then race UNDER the netting between the hulls of the *Great American II*, kind of similar to the way you might ride a skateboard on your belly under a parked tractor trailer—the difference being that if you fell off our floating skateboard, you'd be in sixty feet of cold water in the middle of the night, drunk. With our new and spirited Fourth of July crew, we thought we'd show off and cruise under the *GA II* to demonstrate what fun we were. A sober observer would have recommended against it, but we were six drunks on America's birthday, so fuck you.

As we built up speed and Michael aimed the boat between the trimaran's hulls, I got an inkling that this might be a bad idea. We approached the larger boat and Michael yelled,

"Duck!" One or more of our guests lurched to the side and our boat immediately capsized. We were all in the ocean, fully clothed, in the middle of the night, drunk, and our boat was upside down.

Michael and I struggled mightily to right our dinghy. We couldn't. Even if we could have flipped it over, the motor had filled with saltwater and it was ruined. The best we could do was tie the upside-down dinghy to the stern of the *GA II*. Then, as everyone began to legitimately panic, we decided to climb onto the trimaran to keep from drowning. It was very, very difficult to climb up there. The trimaran didn't have a ladder, nor did it have anything we could easily grab on to. I remember thinking, *"It's possible I'll die in the next few minutes."* After many failed attempts, I managed to propel my body up and out of the water enough to grab on to a railing and pull myself up onto the boat. Everyone was scared, but nobody was screaming or crying or anything. I think they thought Michael and I might somehow know what we were doing, which we very much did not. The water and the fear began to sober us up. Once I was on the boat, I pulled everyone up after me, with the exception of Michael. He had decided he should swim back to the yacht club and get another boat to come save us all, the idea being we might possibly "fix" the situation without getting in trouble with our boss or the police. I, however, was of the opinion that the only important thing was to remain alive. We didn't have a radio and this was a few years before cell phones were pervasive, so our options really were to spend the night on the boat or alternatively, if you were an insane person, swim to shore for help.

Michael and I were drunk, cold, wet, and arguing, and our four passengers were up on the netting of the *Great American II* twiddling their thumbs and likely ruing their decision to join us. I was hanging over the side, pleading with Michael to join us on the boat where we were essentially guaranteed to not die. Swimming across half the harbor during the daytime, in a bathing suit, while sober, would have been challenging enough. Plus the water was less than sixty degrees, which is about forty degrees less than the temperature of, say, a human body. You could hang out in it for a while, but if you didn't get out or drown, you'd ultimately get hypothermia. The swim was at least a quarter of a mile if you traveled in a straight line, and there were respectable waves and a bit of a swell. On top of the current, you would have to swim around boats, so you're absolutely not going in a straight line, thus adding a good amount of yardage to the swim. If you were thrown into the ocean and told you had to swim that distance, you'd be like, "Wow, that's too bad. Oh well, here we go," but you would accomplish it, and you'd have been rightfully proud of yourself. You could say, "I just swam halfway across the harbor," and people would be impressed. At night, when drunk, and fully clothed, including shoes, it was a colossally bad idea.

Michael and I had a screaming debate. He wanted to swim back to the yacht club, go get another launch, pick everybody up, and then try to salvage the launch we'd "borrowed" and very much fucked up.

I said, "Michael, FUCK swimming the harbor! We're all drunk, let's sleep on a comfy boat and flag somebody down in the morning. Who gives a shit if we get yelled at or even fired? We'll be alive."

"I can do it! Let me go!"

"NO, stay here, you could get hypothermia or a wave could go in your mouth and choke you or fucking fifty other things!"

"Don't argue with me, I'm losing strength arguing! I'll be back." Then he just swam off.

I did a quick cost-benefit analysis of jumping in and physically restraining Michael but it seemed like that might kill two people instead of one, and I felt responsibility for the people who were now soaking wet and shivering on the *GA II*, lamenting their decision to hop in a tiny motorboat with a pair of morons.

As Michael swam off, I quickly lost sight of him. I tried to keep our four guests calm, and I told them that Michael would either be back in a bit to pick us up, or he'd die and we'd get picked up the next morning. I was very upset that Michael wasn't on the boat, and that the worst possible outcome wasn't that we were all going to spend a shitty night on a boat—a boat that cost fifty million dollars and was likely comfortable inside but fuck if we knew for sure because we were locked out and would have to spend the night on netting, spooning for warmth, dehydrated, and sobering up until the sun rose and a passing lobsterman radioed my boss or the cops. On top of that, I was sitting there, wondering if my good friend was floating face down, the waves carrying him on his journey toward becoming fish food.

I didn't have a watch on, so I couldn't be sure how long Michael was gone. After what felt like twenty minutes, I started to get worried. Very worried. I imagined telling Michael's dad that he was dead. I knew and loved Michael's dad, so I really indulged that nightmare fantasy, imagining his face and what he would do with a new, raw Michael-shaped hole in his life. I thought, *There's no fucking way he's alive. The best, BEST case scenario is that he got tired, pulled himself up onto another boat, and passed out.* He'd been gone too long and since the errand he was on was fucking incredibly dangerous, he had to be dead. I was totally incapable of spending the night on the boat knowing my friend was dead and I was somewhat responsible. I thought, *He's a fucking idiot cunt stupid head death-wish-having mother-fucker, but why did I allow us to go on the boat ride in the first place? Had it been my idea? Why did I let us pick up those strangers? Was that my idea? Who did what? How? Why? Should I have punched him in the face, knocked him unconscious like in a movie, and then pulled him onto the boat with us? Is he, in fact, correct and 'not getting in trouble' should have been a higher priority for me? Should I have joined him on the swim?* All those thoughts were replaying again and again in my head. I began to scream for help. I remember breathing deep into my belly and trying to scream as loudly and clearly as I possibly could. It wasn't a horror movie scream; it was almost singing. I wanted my scream to reach somebody asleep in a nearby boat, or a police sergeant in his bed, or our boss asleep in his home in Salem, or Michael's dad, or my mom. I bellowed a few times and waited for the sound waves to transform into actual, physical people who could help us. Each "help!" was greeted with silence, or at most, a halyard clanging against a mast or the lapping of little waves on the side of a neighboring boat. Nobody was coming to help. It was pretty distressing to realize that yelling over a comparatively little chunk of ocean at land you can see but not touch is a thoroughly futile exercise.

It was then that I realized Michael was dead. I envisioned the divers who would soon be looking for his body. I'd heard that the harbor was pretty murky, so I wondered if he'd be hard to find. After I genuinely don't know how the fuck long, I heard the familiar sound of one of the Crescent launches starting up from across the harbor at the yacht club. It was FUCKING MUSIC. I saw its running lights turn on. It started to glide across the water and turned toward us. Michael had made it. He pulled alongside the trimaran and I helped our four guests down into the launch. Michael was shivering violently and was sheet-white. He said, "You gotta drive," and collapsed onto the deck. I drove us all back to the club. Our passengers had been blessedly docile during our purgatorial stay on the *Great American II*. I think we were collectively ashamed of our stupidity and eye-contact or talking became painful after a certain point. I took Michael to the pier house and closed the door. He was pre-hypothermic, dehydrated, and a mess. I made him lie on the ground and I got on top of him and pulled my shirt up so I could heat his body. I held him for a bit, very, VERY excited to have him alive and in my arms. I knew there'd be consequences of some kind to follow, be they medical, professional, or even legal, but I absolutely didn't care since I had been STONE certain that he was dead a half an hour earlier.

Once he warmed back up, we realized that we were lying down hugging with no shirts on while four strangers milled about outside the door. We'd have told them to fuck off back to wherever they came from, but the dock of the Crescent was miles from where we'd picked them up, so they were waiting for us to drive them (drunk) back to their car.

To this day that embrace between Michael and me remains the only time I've snuggled shirtless with another man while in a lying-down position after consuming fifteen beers. I remember it fondly, and I'd do it again. After Michael came back to a more functional version of life and some color had returned to his skin, we went out again in the launch to retrieve the dinghy. When we got to the trimaran, we still couldn't flip the dinghy back over, so we wound up towing it slowly back to the dock upside down. Any safety gear or tools that had been in the dinghy floated away or sank into the darkness. We'd both lost our shoes. When we made it back to the dock, we tied up both the boats—the dinghy still upside down—and then drove our bewildered passengers back to their cars on the mainland. We never saw them again.

The next day, our boss was, naturally, irate. He laid into Michael and me, and I was ashamed. We'd done something indefensible and nearly fatal, and we'd done it with boats and equipment he had built and maintained. Michael and I brought the outboard motor to a shop to be drained, fixed, relubricated, and repaired. That was the biggest physical casualty of the night. More than that though, our genuinely beloved boss had proof that we were total assholes and as dependable as ham sandwiches. He was sincerely disappointed and I felt like shit about it. He couldn't easily fire us, though, because to get the job in the first place we had to get Coast Guard and Merchant Marines–issued licenses to drive the launches. Those licenses required many hours of training, classes, tests, and drug testing. We were not easily replaceable and there were simply too many passengers that would need transport in the coming months. So Bill sucked it up and kept us.

One month later exactly, on August fourth, I was taking a load of people back to the Crescent on one of the launches. I saw a shoe floating in the water. I pulled alongside it and picked it up. It was an ugly white size thirteen Sperry boat sneaker. Amazingly, it was one of the shoes that I'd lost a month prior, when I kicked it off in an effort to not drown. I put the shoe at the base of my seat, stunned, and drove my passengers back to the club.

That night in 1998 was only one of the many incidents where my drinking could have had fatal consequences, but I shrugged it off and kept truckin'. I was scared of what could or would happen—I was never intellectually unaware of the danger I put myself in; I just loved to drink. And the distance from one drink to eight or fifteen was like a waterslide or a well-lit path in a very alluring wood.

So, after I got back to the club and threw my shoe in the trash I made plans to do what I did best after my shift ended, and got loaded.

le courage

One night in the summer of 1999 I jumped off the Manhattan
Bridge. It wasn't a suicide attempt; I had a bungee cord attached to my ankles. But it was still illegal and not part of any
tour package or team-building exercise.

I'd just graduated from NYU and was working as a waiter at
the Atlantic Grill on the Upper East Side. Right before I graduated, I booked the role of Sir Lancelot in a touring company
of *Camelot*, but the tour didn't begin rehearsals until fall, so I
spent the summer waiting tables. The night in question, I ate
probably twenty-five pieces of exotic sushi that patrons had left
untouched on their plates. Rich people ate at the restaurant

and thought nothing of ordering two hundred dollars' worth of sushi and eating half of it. What was I supposed to do, not eat it?

At around eleven, I split up my tips with the busboys, then headed out and took the 6 train back to Alphabet City, planning to drink a twelve-pack of Lowenbrau without assistance.

When I got back to my apartment my roommate, Kiyash, was pacing around and smiling.

"Guess what I'm gonna do tonight?" he asked.

"What?"

"I'm gonna bungee-jump off the Manhattan Bridge!"

I'd met Kiyash during my junior year in Paris. I was drawn to him immediately because he was a smart, fun, well-read guy who was always up for an adventure. He was named for an island in the Persian Gulf off of Iran, which is where his father Manouchehr was born. Manouchehr had an archetypal entrance to the United States in 1963 when the boat that took him across the Atlantic encountered fog as it approached land. After a period of very low visibility, the Statue of Liberty herself emerged from the fog, looming over their boat, welcoming them to the United States.

Rather than ask Kiyash any questions (like, WHY ARE YOU JUMPING OFF THE MANHATTAN BRIDGE?) I told him I was coming with him and we headed out the door to meet "some guy who has a bungee cord" near the Brooklyn on-ramp to the Manhattan Bridge. Kiyash didn't know the cord owner, but he did know a Polish guy who knew him, so we went to meet his friend Dariusz at a bar.

I didn't know Dariusz, but he endeared himself to me by immediately launching into a story about how he'd learned the hard way earlier that day that wearing a tiny Speedo bathing suit to the beach draws a lot of attention in the U.S. He presented Kiyash and me with a cogent argument as to why Speedo suits are superior and why American men were silly for not wearing them. We told him he'd made a great case but that American women tended to prefer a little mystery where a man's junk dimensions were concerned, even though solving such a mystery might involve facing down a disappointing penis lurking in the shadow of a fat gut after drinking a bucket of wine coolers at a rented beach house. Dariusz was pretty fit though, so I'm sure his ensemble made some people happy.

After bonding with Dariusz, we headed out to meet the guy who'd show us how to jump off a bridge.

About fifteen people were gathered on a busy corner of Flatbush Avenue waiting for the guy with the rope. For something wholly illegal and intrinsically dangerous, it was a rather well advertised operation. After a few minutes, "Tony" arrived and led us along Flatbush Avenue toward the on-ramp to the bridge. As we traveled, Tony gave us instructions, including the order to "lie down" if the subway passed us on the bridge so the conductors wouldn't see us. Tony had me carry the bungee cord up the bridge in a big bag. It weighed maybe fifty pounds and I told myself its substantial weight meant it must be really safe. When we'd covered some distance, he handed out walkietalkies set to the police frequency to a few of the "customers" (he'd asked us to give him twenty dollars apiece). He told us to listen for any discussion among the cops about a "large group of people sneaking out onto the Manhattan Bridge with crazy gear." He said that it'd be hard to get away if they wanted to arrest us, so what we were really listening for was for any mention of Truck 2 or Truck 6. He said that those names referred to "tactical antiterrorist units that would kill us first and then figure out who we were." He said if we heard that those groups were being sent to the bridge, we should just drop everything, run, and not stop until we were in New Jersey. I listened very carefully for Trucks 2 and 6 for the next few hours.

We walked out over the East River, hitting the deck whenever a train came by, and made it about one-eighth of a mile from the Brooklyn shore, then set up our station. Our first instructions from Tony were to climb down a level on the bridge and, I swear to God, disable the red lights that hang from the bridge to alert airplanes, "Hello. I am a bridge." I'm sure that today, after 9/11, New York law enforcement would "Truck 6" your ass off for that stunt, but our adventure took place two years prior to the attacks, so we didn't imagine anyone would be too upset that we were turning a piece of vital metropolitan infrastructure into an amusement park ride and making it partially invisible to air traffic.

Then Tony, who claimed to be a "theatrical rigger," took out the bungee cord and secured it to something. To what? To a piece of bridge, I guess. I have no idea. Tony then asked who wanted to go first and a short guy with a buzz cut volunteered.

Before he let the test subject jump, Tony thrust a tape recorder in the guy's face.

"WHAT IS YOUR NAME?"

"DAVE!"

"WHAT ARE YOU ABOUT TO DO?"

"JUMP OFF THE MANHATTAN BRIDGE!"

"ARE YOU DOING THIS OF YOUR OWN VOLI-
TION?"

"YES!"

"JUMP!"

The guy jumped, screaming. It was loud for a fraction of a
second, then immediately much quieter, as though someone
had very quickly turned a volume knob down. The reason his
screaming got quieter, to us, is that he had just jumped off a
bridge. I looked over the edge and he had disappeared into the
black. Disabling the bridge's lights had effectively shrouded us
in inky darkness. I very sincerely believed the rope had broken
and he had gone into the river. I was certain I'd helped facili-
tate the death of someone. Someone stupid, like me.

But then Tony yelled, "You all right down there?" and the
test subject meowed a weak "Yes."

Then a cop car pulled up at the water's edge in Brooklyn.

There was no activity on the scanners, but Tony yell-
whispered down to Jumper One, "Just chill out for a second;
don't move." Kiyash and I looked at each other, incredulous.
Don't move? What if his head filled with blood and exploded?
How long can a person hang upside down without passing out
or becoming permanently stupid? What if Truck 6 fired a mis-
sile up his defenseless asshole?

After a few terrifying minutes, the cop left, not having seen

us. We threw another rope with a carabiner down to Danglin'
Dave, he hooked it onto his waist, and we manually pulled him
back up to the bridge. I calculated that he probably weighed
seventy-five percent of what I weighed, so there was probably
a three out of four chance I'd survive. He said, "Whoa" a bunch
in a manner that suggested he was properly awed but not necessarily retarded after the rush of blood to his head. Good
enough for me!

Then it was my turn. Though I counted maybe eleven reasons as to why I shouldn't jump, several of them potentially
fatal or crippling, and all of them criminal, I was determined to
have a stranger tie a rope around my ankles and leap off that
bridge at three in the morning, as planned.

Tony stuck his tape recorder in my face.

"WHAT IS YOUR NAME?"

"ROB DELANEY."

(I must point out that Kiyash made fun of me without inter-
ruption for several years at how much naked fear was audible in
my shaky high-pitched voice as I answered Tony's questions.)

"WHAT ARE YOU ABOUT TO DO?"

"JUMP OFF THE MANHATTAN BRIDGE!"

"ARE YOU DOING THIS OF YOUR OWN VOLI-
TION?"

"YES!"

"JUMP!"

I jumped.

I looked out over a sleepy, twinkling Manhattan as I plum-
meted into the night. It was wonderful and visceral, like my

mind and body were violently wiped clean and rebooted to take in the majesty of the experience. It felt like a reverse birth as I flew into and through the darkness toward the river. Then the slack in the cord tightened as my rocketing mass stretched it to its limit and I shot skyward (and bridgeward) almost as fast as I'd descended. I made it almost to the bridge, then fell again and began a series of bounces. It was like being in a giant glitter globe as the city's lights shook around me. I felt entirely buoyed and supported and loved by the dirty river, the ugly bridge, the beautiful city, and the questionable rope. Then Tony threw down the "yank 'em up" rope, and after it swung past me a few times I was able to grab it, hook it to my waist, and get pulled back to the bridge by my fellow jumpers.

Then Kiyash and the others jumped, one by one, and we pulled them back up. We packed up as the sun rose and took the train home to Alphabet City to sleep, arriving in full day-light. It had been entirely magnificent to watch about twenty people in a row have an experience you knew they'd talk about for the rest of their lives, and participate in it as well. It was interesting to see the few people who backed out so totally at peace with their decision too.

Nobody gave them a hard time either; I know I thought, *"Of course you don't want to JUMP OFF A BRIDGE. Why would anyone do that? That would be crazy."* Those of us who had jumped were pretty much aglow. As my reflections began to gather and coalesce in my brain, I was absolutely glad I had done it, but I knew I would never do it again. Nor would I allow a loved one, or really anyone, to do it, since I'd seen how ramshackle an operation it was. It was a singular rush and an extraordinarily terrible idea, all at once.

And while I have difficulty imagining a scenario where I'd do something that reckless again, I'm very happy I can say I jumped off the Manhattan Bridge and you, statistically, cannot.

nu et sanglant

When given a choice where to spend my downtime, I will rarely pick a jail, psychiatric hospital, or halfway house. While that is true now, for a few months when I was twenty-five, I called those places home.

Twelve years ago I was in jail, in a wheelchair. The hospital gown I was in was covered in blood from my bleeding face. My top front right tooth was missing a piece. My right arm and my left wrist were broken. They were broken so badly they both required surgery. My knees were fucked up too. They'd slammed into the dashboard of the car I was driving the night before and split open to the bone. They weren't broken but they'd been operated on and sewed shut in the emergency room of Cedars-Sinai hospital, just before I went to jail. They were in leg stabilizers, which are reinforced fabric, Velcro, and steel leg braces that don't let you bend your knees. So, since I couldn't use my arms to grip the wheelchair's armrests, or bend my knees to steady myself on the ground, I would occasionally slip down and fall out of my wheelchair onto the floor of my cell. As I slid down the chair to the floor, my gown would fly open and my dick, balls, and even my defenseless little asshole were exposed to everyone in jail. If you've been to jail or read a book about it or seen any movies about it, you know you're supposed to keep that shit to yourself. A kindly couple of cops would usually help me back into my wheelchair, then I'd slip right out a little while later. Not because I wanted to show everyone my dick and balls and asshole but because I couldn't use my arms or legs.

The night before, I'd driven a car into the side of a branch office of the Los Angeles Department of Water and Power. It wasn't even my car. A few days prior, I'd been in another accident, albeit a minor one. I was at a stoplight and someone slammed into my 1988 Volvo wagon from behind, inflicting enough damage that it required the car spend a few days in the shop. As such, for my second, larger accident, I was driving a brand-new white Nissan Altima, which happened to be equipped with an airbag. Based on the damage that my arms and legs sustained as they hit the front of the car, and based on the broken tooth and bloodied face I received from the airbag, a feature my fourteen-year-old Volvo did not have, it is entirely possible that the gentleman who hit me from behind three days earlier had, in fact, saved my life. I remember when we exchanged information seeing that his name was "Ivan Dearman." Ivan, you are indeed a dear man, and I am profoundly grateful you were distracted by a phone call or a Bacardi billboard and hit me from behind that morning in February 2002.

A few nights later, I was driving the white Altima that Ivan Dearman's insurance paid for. I was very, very drunk and, on my way to the Department of Water and Power, I took out four parking meters, two trees, and a light post.

Here's the order of the events: I was at a keg party at a friend's house. There were maybe forty people there. I drank beer for a few hours. My only memories of the party are meeting a beautiful woman named Djuna and talking about the Djuna Barnes book *Nightwood*, and then kissing a different beautiful woman who was a friend of mine that I'd always wanted to kiss.

The keg got drained, so I started drinking wine. After we (I) finished the wine, I moved on to liquor. Although I'd thought about quitting drinking for years, I pretty much as a rule would start with beer and would stick with it until it was gone or I passed out. But if the beer ran out and I was still conscious, I would continue to drink whatever was around. My last memory before blacking out was filling a big red Solo cup up to the top with bourbon, vodka, and ice. If you're not a drinker, bourbon and vodka on ice is not actually a drink. I'm reminded of the Ozzy Osbourne song "Suicide Solution." Nobody drinks bourbon mixed with vodka unless they're pledging a fraternity, lamenting the friends they lost in combat, or are what doctors call a "garden variety alcoholic." I drank that down like it was lemonade on a hot day, then filled the cup again with my proprietary blend. As that second cup touched my lips, my memory stopped working.

Over the coming months, I found out that after draining the second Solo cup, I'd passed out on my friend's floor. Everyone else either left or went to bed. Then I apparently "woke up" in the middle of a blackout and went for a drive. For the uninitiated, a blackout is when you're so drunk that your long-term memory is effectively disabled. So you can function in the moment (albeit in a very impaired manner), but you wake up the next day with minutes or hours missing, never to be found again except in the memories of the people unfortunate enough to have witnessed your antics. People kill their friends, family, and strangers in blackouts all the time. They're a nasty business, and for a little over a decade, I experienced them all the time.

I am not sure of the route I took in my blackout drive but I wound up crashing the car somewhere quite far from both the party and my apartment. I don't remember any of the drive, the accident, or the extraction from the vehicle and subsequent ambulance ride to Cedars-Sinai hospital. That is probably for the best. I do remember being wheeled into the emergency room though, strapped down to the gurney by all four appendages and my head. When I came to, I was hallucinating and believed Nazi doctors had kidnapped me and were going to experiment on me. If you've seen the film *Jacob's Ladder*, in which Tim Robbins's tortured Vietnam vet character is wheeled around a nightmare hospital with horned nurses and doctors with no eyes, then you understand the type of situation I believed I was in. My plan was to act like I was "okay with it" and that being in the Nazi hospital was no big deal, but as soon as I got the "lay of the land" I planned to figure out how to escape (even though I couldn't move a single part of my body).

VERY gradually, I began to gather that the doctors and nurses were actually trying to help me and that I was, in fact, responsible for my current circumstances. There were two cops accompanying me wherever the hospital staff wheeled me, and we chatted a bit whenever I could croak out a question or answer. It took me a while to work up the courage to ask them if I'd killed anyone. I decided that if the answer were yes, I'd kill myself at the earliest opportunity. When they told me I hadn't, every molecule in my body and mind surrendered and I was, in a way, almost happy.

I had been trying to quit drinking for many years with no success, so I was almost immediately glad I'd gotten so fucked up by the accident. Now there was NO way to hide that I was a disastrous, dangerous, ridiculous alcoholic piece of shit. I looked like what I'd felt like for years. Up to then, I had success hiding it from some people, some of the time. Now, though, I was a bloody, broken mess of a person and it was obvious, even from a distance, at night, from across the street, in the rain, that there was a LOT that was wrong with me.

My history with drunk driving was not as long as one might

imagine, given that I'd been drinking since I was twelve. During high school and visits home to Marblehead during college, I would occasionally drive drunk. But since I went to college in New York City, I didn't have a car, thus the number of people I could potentially kill at any moment was lower than that of a person who was habitually drunk behind a wheel. As long as I thought I was the only person who might wind up dead as a result of my drinking, I was happy to continue on course.

But when I moved to L.A. and got a car I realized, "Shit, I drink and drive a lot." I was ashamed of this fact and made a half-assed effort not to do it, but as you see, I was not at all successful.

A few months before driving into the Department of Water and Power, I decided, for maybe the twenty-fifth time in my life, to quit drinking. Here's why: I had attended my friend Dan's wedding in France on September 9, 2001. He married an actual countess and the wedding and reception took place at her family's chateau in Bordeaux. It was the most opulent celebration I've ever attended, on grounds a little larger than a medium-sized college campus. An American Airlines stewardess propositioned me at the reception and I politely said no because I'd wanted to get it on with a Lithuanian friend of the bride who had light green eyes. To use an old Lithuanian saying, she "wasn't interested," so I slept alone that night.

I'd traveled to France from the U.S. with my friend Jon, a mutual friend of the groom. In high school, Jon was painfully cool and older than me and we didn't really know each other well. After high school we'd bump into each other when he'd visit from his college in Santa Fe and I'd visit from New York. We both liked to read and drink and chase girls, so we hit it off. The day after the wedding, Jon and I took a smoke-filled train to Paris, where I was fortunate enough to know a few people, having spent my junior year of college there. On the afternoon of September eleventh—at which time it was morning in New York City—Jon and I were exploring the catacombs several stories beneath the streets of Montparnasse.

In the eighteenth century, when the city's graveyards had begun to overflow, millions of folks' remains were gathered and brought deep underground to a series of tunnels and methodically stacked. It's peaceful down there, walking through hallways lined with stacks of femurs accented here and there by a heart or a cross made of skulls. It strikes me that we were surrounded by thousands of peaceful dead during the attacks of September eleventh.

When Jon and I emerged from the catacombs, we went to a travel agent's office to buy plane tickets to Krakow. We were planning to stay with a friend I'd met a couple of years earlier. As we sat opposite the travel agent's desk, he asked us if we'd heard that a plane had hit the World Trade Center, causing it to collapse. I sincerely thought that he didn't have a firm grasp on the English language and was trying to tell us something else, something that wasn't an incomprehensible nightmare. I made him tell me again, in French, and he confirmed that he had in fact meant to say that the World Trade Center was no longer two buildings that stood 110 stories high in lower Manhattan. I thought he was either crazy or was repeating something he'd been told by some other moron. We actually finished buying our tickets, thinking we'd call home and find out that all was well. When we left the office, people were gathered around news kiosks. Something terribly out of the ordinary had indeed happened.

Jon and I were able to squeeze out a call each to our respective families before the transatlantic lines were totally swamped. I spoke to my mom and we were as scared as anyone, but I found some solace in knowing that she wasn't near any of the day's nightmare events. I asked her to try to get in touch with a couple of my friends who lived in downtown Manhattan. After that, we couldn't dependably get through to the U.S. for a few days. We went back to our hosts' apartment and watched the towers fall on the news. Then we went out and got drunk.

The next day we flew to Poland. NOBODY wanted to fly, so we had a pretty big plane to ourselves. We stayed with my friend Marta and had a stunned, shitty time.

After a few days, we returned to Paris. From there, Jon traveled east and ultimately spent six months working his way from Italy to southeast Asia and on to New Zealand. He kept the first "blog" I ever read, which was wonderful.

After Jon left, I stayed in Paris for a few more days, doing no small amount of drinking. I also—no joke—looked into the logistics of joining the French Foreign Legion. I knew the United States would respond in some way to 9/11 and I had an idea that I might not be in agreement with their approach. I wanted to be up to speed on how to join the legendary Legion, which is famous for accepting any able-bodied person from anywhere in the world, training them, deploying them wherever they see fit, then furnishing them with a French passport if they perform admirably. Of course, I didn't want to join any army, but if we descended into global war, I at least wanted to avail myself of the option of not being cannon fodder for George W. Bush and his execrable cabinet.

I learned that to gain entry to the Legion you had to be able to do at least thirty push-ups and ten pull-ups. So I made sure I could do that and more. I already spoke passable French. In retrospect, it sounds somewhat crazy, but it also sounds entirely sane when, eighteen months after 9/11, the U.S. invaded Iraq because a few blood- and oil-thirsty neocon monsters felt like it. Like many others, I was sick when the U.S. entered Iraq. Afghanistan, sure; they thought they'd rustle up the folks who planned the attacks of 9/11. Whether you agreed with it or not, you could follow the thought process. Iraq, however, was and is a black, bloody blot on our nation's very recent history. May shame haunt the people who beat the drum for that manufactured war from now until they die in a comfortable hospital bed paid for by your taxes.

In addition to my calisthenics to prepare for possible Legion basic training, I drank. My first flight scheduled to take me back to the U.S. was canceled. American Airlines was unbelievably accommodating and essentially said, "Fly WHENEVER you want! We are so very grateful that anyone would consider flying after what's happened that you just say the word, Mr. Delaney!" With that leeway, I pushed my departure date back a few days. Then I got so drunk the night before I was scheduled to leave that I slept through my alarm and missed it.

"Not a problem, Mr. Delaney! You just fly whenever it suits you! Think of your ticket as a coupon entitling you to fly at your whim, without restrictions! Miss a flight and don't feel like calling to postpone or cancel? Fret not! Show up whenever you like."

One night before I left, I went out drinking with my friend Yacine. After hitting a few bars, we were both drunk, and Yacine made the fantastic decision to go home and go to bed. I decided to stay out. I got profoundly drunk and at one point was sitting on a curb just off the Champs-Elysees. Why I was there, I have no idea. The Champs-Elysees is the equivalent of Fifth Avenue; it's a place to throw money in the garbage can at expensive shops, not a place to enjoy nightlife and certainly not a place for career alcoholics to get any serious drinking done.

In any case, while I was sitting alongside the Champs-Elysees, a large black Mercedes pulled up and a guy in a suit asked me if I needed a ride. I said yes and I GOT IN A STRANGE MAN'S MERCEDES AT TWO O'CLOCK IN THE MORNING IN A LARGE METROPOLIS.

He asked me if I wanted to go to a bar with him. I did! We went to one bar and I had a drink or two. When I went to pay with a credit card, the bartender ran it and said it didn't work. He asked if I had another. The second one worked, according to him.

Then the Mercedes man took me to another bar. After a few minutes of observing the clientele at this second, much nicer bar, I realized it was attached to a brothel and it was filled with prostitutes. That made me uncomfortable, so I got up to leave. I realized that the door was blocked by a man who was the size of another door, so I sat back down again. A hooker sat next to me and asked me if I wanted to retire with her to a private room. Drunk as I was, I told her no thanks. I paid for my drinks and—get this—my credit card (which worked everywhere else I'd used it) didn't work, so I gave the bartender another one, which worked. Then I asked Mr. Mercedes if I could leave. He said yes and that he'd give me a ride. I really didn't want one, but I was very drunk and, at this point, afraid. Also, I had no idea where we were. I gave him an address to drop me off at, and, thank Jesus, he did. That address was of course nowhere near where I was actually staying because I didn't want him to murder my hosts or be able to find me again for another early morning joyride.

Several weeks later, back in Los Angeles, I got two credit card bills in the mail that were fascinatingly huge. I'd apparently spent several thousand dollars on the four or five drinks I bought at the two bars Mr. Mercedes took me to. Nice work! I called one credit card company and told them someone must have stolen my information.

While technically an agreement with a credit card company probably protects you from things like weirdo scam artists consciously overcharging you to steal money from you, I didn't really want to explain to them, "Well, you see, I had been drunk for several days and then one night I got in a stranger's car and he took me to a brothel where, you must believe me, I did not procure sexual favors from a prostitute. The charge on my card is not for sex, no sir." So I just lied and said I had no idea what that big charge was from and they said, "Okay," and took it off.

The second credit card company said, "Fuck off. Pay it, you weird drunk liar." To which I replied, "Can do!"

So, since I got stuck with a roughly two-thousand-dollar hit as a consequence of getting blind drunk and then accepting a ride from a stranger in a foreign city who drove me to a brothel where I was robbed in a truly twenty-first-century fashion, I decided it was time to take a break from the booze. It was just such an odd confluence of shitty, dangerous, costly things at once that it put into stark clarity, once again, the fact that I was bad at drinking and very, very good at making terrible decisions once drunk.

Also, when I got back from Paris, my uncle Burt died. He was my dad's younger brother and he was an alcoholic. He was on a train on his way from Boston to New Jersey to visit my cousin when he had a heart attack and died at age fifty. He was the youngest of four, the other three of whom are still alive today. He and my dad and their other brother and sister grew up poor in Boston and I know that they shared a bed as kids and took care of each other in foster homes and orphanages. Though their parents were alive, their mother left their father after Burt's birth and there was a period of some years when their father couldn't afford to keep everyone under one roof and fed and clothed. Is that why Burt drank? I suspect it was just because he was an alcoholic. None of the other three kids had issues with substances, including my dad. While I'm no doctor, my own field research suggests substance abuse derives a little more from nature than nurture. Situations can exacerbate it, but alcoholism affects the rich and the poor, morons and the brilliant. My uncle Burt drank and died young; my dad didn't and he's pushing seventy and lives by the ocean on Cape Ann.

Burt was a carpenter and I can remember enjoying going to the fridge as a little kid and getting a Michelob for him when he worked on our house. Michelobs were fun to open because their cap was covered with paper that you had to tear as you opened the bottle. I liked to draw and paint when I was a boy, and one day my uncle Burt made me a frame out of extra two-by-fours to use for my art. I was so young that when he handed me the square frame I told him, "Thank you, Uncle Burt, but I do my paintings on rectangular paper," to which he replied, "You can cut paper to make it square and then it'll fit."

"Wow, that's a great idea!" was my response to that. YOU CAN CUT/TEAR PAPER THEREBY CHANGING ITS SIZE/DIMENSIONS. This was news to me. So it could be argued that my uncle Burt opened up whole new artistic vistas to me at that moment.

His passing certainly opened my eyes. Burt was the only relative I'd watched deteriorate and die from alcoholism and it drove home for me the realization that if I looked back at my drinking and then extrapolated potential future scenarios, a heart attack on a train was among the more desirable possibilities. And that still sounded like a shit option.

So I decided to quit drinking. Smoking pot, however, I

would continue, and I'd dial up my intake so that I could still be intoxicated in some fashion every day. By the time I got the brothel statement, I was such a dedicated drinker that the idea of quitting all mind-altering substances didn't seem possible. I did not like being sober, particularly around other people. So I smoked pot every day, played a lot of Pac-Man, and was very miserable. I can remember being unhappy all the time and thinking, *"At least I'm not drinking."*

Then my twenty-fifth birthday arrived and I decided to have a birthday party. I invited everyone I knew. I had it at a restaurant in Los Feliz called Tangier that had a big back room in which a respectable crowd could dance. About twenty or thirty people came and it was a lot of fun. I remember watching Eli Roth, who would one day write and direct *Cabin Fever* and the brutal *Hostel* films, dancing like a sweaty madman and laughing. As the small hours of the early morning approached and the bar began to close, I noticed a tiny, fair-skinned woman with a short black bob haircut and severe bangs at a corner table. When I looked at her, she didn't look away. I approached and saw that she was entirely fetching, so I introduced myself. She was Austrian and in L.A. working as an architect. We had an easy chat and at the end of it, she let me have her phone number. I acted like I wasn't excited, but I certainly was. I called her the next day and asked her if she'd let me take her out and she said yes. I immediately got nervous as I considered the prospect of trying to interact with an attractive woman one-on-one without the aid of alcohol. So even though I hadn't had a drink in several weeks, when I took her to dinner a couple of nights later, we shared a bottle of wine, then went to a bar and had more drinks.

I didn't get drunk, but when we went back to my apartment and had sex, I thought, *"There's no way I could have done that without alcohol."* I took it as a sign that it was okay for me to start drinking again. And drink again I did. The next two weeks were very frightening because I drank a little more each day and could really feel my appetite for booze surging in strength. Though I'd had no shortage of problems with alcohol in the past, I had never been able to feel the unquenchable desire to get and stay blind drunk so strongly and consistently. It made my body feel hot and I had thoughts whose intensity bordered on hallucination where my ribs were the bars of a jail cell and my urge to drink and just bludgeon my consciousness took the form of a demon inside of me, not begging to get out, but rather growing in strength until it burst out of the cage as a matter of course. It was terrifying. I saw the Austrian woman again two more times and managed to not scare her. She was lovely and kind and would have probably made someone in better shape a good girlfriend. But I wasn't able to entertain that possibility since my top priority was getting drunk. Fifteen days after my birthday party I went to the keg party earlier that would land me in Cedars-Sinai's ER following the aforementioned violent detour where my rented Nissan Altima so passionately kissed a branch office of the Los Angeles Department of Water and Power.

In the emergency room they checked me out reasonably well. They pinched and squeezed me and said, "Does this hurt?" all over my body. I said no every time, because I was still so fucked up that nothing did hurt. Subsequent hospital visits would reveal that both my left wrist and right arm were broken; my right ulna was effectively smashed. But I felt fine at the time, so they left it at that. My forehead was scraped off from the airbag, which caused me to bleed all over my hospital gown and, as I mentioned, both my knees were cut open from hitting the dashboard. There was a resident helping the head ER doctor fix me up, and he sewed up my right knee while the head doctor was out of the room.

When the doctor came back he said to the resident, "Wow, you really fucked that one up. It's all zigzaggy. That's going to be a horrible scar. Try to do a better job on the other one." That's my first clear memory as I gradually came back to consciousness. And the resident did do a better job; one of my knees has a jagged, abstract-art scar and one of them has a nice straight line. I would later receive the clothes they cut me out of in a trash bag. They were soaked with blood.

After the stitches and medical tests, the cops took me to jail. By this point the booze had started to wear off and my arms were beginning to let me know they were broken by sending strong, clear waves of pain through my body. Any use of my right arm produced an audible crunching and clicking. It also had what looked like an extra elbow bulging out of the middle of my forearm. They wheeled me into the police station to book me. You're supposed to be standing when they fingerprint you, but I could not, so an officer lifted my arms above my head and onto the table. I screamed in pain.

I wasn't in jail for that long, a few hours at most. I would have been there for a few days, but I was too much of a pain in the ass so they just folded me in half and put me in the back of a cruiser and drove me home. They actually drove by the junk-yard on the way home so I could get some stuff out of my rental car. The car was utterly destroyed. It was fully caved in on the front and back and half the size it had been the day before. You'd have thought it was a washing machine or a stove if you didn't know it was a car.

As the cops escorted me into my apartment, I shuffled past my building manager and assured her, "It's okay, I'm fine!" though I was rather obviously the opposite of fine. I was still in the bloody hospital gown and was wearing the metal-reinforced leg stabilizers so I looked like a partially finished, emaciated Frankenstein. I thanked the cops for the ride and crawled onto my bed.

A few hours later, I woke up to take a piss and was surprised to discover that my urine was neon blue. Though I'd grown used to being totally horrified by myself at this point, this was especially upsetting. I started to cry at the sight. After crying for a bit, I needed to blow my nose. When I did so, bits of broken glass came out with the snot. Bits of windshield were still up there. That made me even more scared and I started to get hot and hyperventilate. I took off the hospital gown and was further shocked to discover stickers all over my body. Upon examination, it turned out they weren't decorative; they were the little anchors for heart monitor wires that I'd been hooked up to. They were all over my hairy body and they took forever to peel off with my broken arms. More stickers would turn up over the coming days that I'd missed on the first search-and-remove mission. And the blue piss was a byproduct of the methylene blue they'd flushed my system with. They do that to see if you're hemorrhaging internally. Thankfully, I was not.

Naturally, there was a court date coming up that I needed to get ready for. I got a lawyer and my saintly uncle Steve flew out from Boston to help me for a few days and get everything in order. Steve is one of my mom's older brothers, and is a wonderful guy. I didn't even ask him; he just flew out when he heard what had happened. I'd spoken to him on several occasions in the past about my desire to quit drinking, so the news that I'd driven into a building didn't surprise him. My parents didn't come and I'm glad of that. I wouldn't have wanted them to see me in such disrepair. And Steve didn't ask; he just came. It was really quite a Navy Seal move. Uncle smells trouble; deploys immediately to help without asking permission. Hot shit if you ask me.

The lawyer recommended I go directly to rehab and throw myself at the mercy of the judge, pleading no contest. Rehab sounded like a great idea, so a few days after the accident I moved into the chemical dependency unit of Las Encinas Hospital in Pasadena for the standard twenty-eight-day period, hoping my health insurance would cover it. I didn't have regular employment at the time; just a hodgepodge of babysitting, catering, and working in a furniture store warehouse, so none of them would miss me. I told a few friends I'd be away for a bit and they were uniformly kind and concerned. When my court date rolled around, I'd already been in rehab for a week. While that proactive move may have helped reduce the severity of my sentence, I truly didn't want to be anywhere else on earth than a Rehab with a capital R.

The grounds of Las Encinas are beautiful and are actually designated as a registered arboretum by the state of California. The hospital itself is home to crazy people whose lives had gotten to the point that they needed a little "time-out" and the opportunity to regroup with the help of medicine and doctors. I fit right the fuck in, and I was once again grateful my outsides matched my insides for the first time in a long time. My brain and heart had developed some kinks that were killing me and I knew they needed straightening.

I met some very nice schizophrenics at Las Encinas, women with postpartum depression, people with split personalities, and then "regular" folks who were mentally healthy but had had too many tragedies befall them at once for them to keep it all together and act like everything was okay. And I remember them fondly. One very nice man, who was just under seven feet tall, liked to wear a very realistic bear mask when he went to the dining hall. He talked normally and was entirely pleasant. He just liked to wear a bear mask.

The hottest girl in the whole hospital (and the one I developed a slight crush on) was in there because she'd killed a guy and was in for observation. But as human beings, whatever social situation we're in, we just sort of organize people in our minds and play games with ourselves like, "If I *had* to have sex with someone here, it would be . . ." Well, this was the most extreme example of that so far in my life; there were a bunch of people in my social circle, which HAPPENED to be a mental hospital, and one chick had to be the hottest, and in this case she was a killer. It's not my fault that she wore tight sweatpants all the time and did her hair all nice.

Then there was Rhonda. Rhonda was about fifty and she was there because she'd jumped off a roof. Well, that's part of why she was there. One day I saw her on the lawn and said, "Hi Rhonda!"

"Excusez-moi?" she said.

"Hello?"

Then she goes, "I am sorry, I do not speak English. I am from France."

Now, it so happens that I actually speak French and I thought about just continuing speaking with her new "French" personality, but JUST IN CASE her "French" personality didn't actually speak French I didn't want to make her head explode, so I just said, "Okay, have a nice day!" and walked away.

And those were just the people I'd see in the dining hall. I spent the bulk of my days and nights with the people in the chemical dependency unit, which was called Briar. They were my brethren: the drunks, junkies, tweakers, coke addicts, pill poppers, and crackheads. They were truck drivers, executives, housewives, producers, grandmas, and nurses. They were black, white, Jewish, Asian, Italian, and Mexican. The thing that united us is that we loved to get fucked up and were all very good at it. Our days were spent in groups of various sizes, talking, sharing, and learning how to live life without drugs and alcohol. I was sort of a mascot for the place because I was the most visibly fucked-up person there. I was extremely skinny. My right arm was in a big cast and my left arm was in a brace. While at Las Encinas I took a field trip to a "normal" hospital to have a plate and seven screws put into my right arm. Once that healed, my doctor planned to fuse the bone I'd broken in my left wrist. One of my fonder memories remains the day I knew I'd broken my right arm and the doctor came in to tell me I'd broken my left wrist as well and both would require debilitating surgery that would require months of recovery and occupational therapy. I calmly asked him to leave the room so I could cry by myself.

Muscle atrophy and lack of appetite accounted for my rail-thin frame. I limped, too, because my right ankle had been damaged in the accident. And with my arms in casts, it was too hard for me to use pants pockets, so I wore a black canvas workman's vest that had two big pockets on the front that I could keep stuff in. It looked sad, like maybe I ran a craft workshop for runaways out of my broken-down van in a parking lot by a beach.

Despite my appearance, the saddest people in the place were still the junkies. Watching all of them kick heroin and painkillers was the worst. They basically just shake and kick all day and night for days. I learned to never go into the bathroom after one of them had been in there. After a kicking junkie has taken a shit in a bathroom it looks like a baby elephant has been hosed off after playing in a muddy riverbank all day. There were various group therapy meetings at Las Encinas that were not unlike what they show on TV and in movies. One night somebody thought it would be fun to watch the movie *28 Days*, in which Sandra Bullock goes to rehab. I was rather disturbed when one of the film's major characters—named *Delaney*—RELAPSES AND DIES.

My mental state at the time was entirely fight-or-flight. I was in shock that I was alive and I knew that everything would be changing thoroughly and often, so I sort of walled off sections of my psyche and compartmentalized, not really letting myself feel or experience anything on too deep of a level. I was on guard and cautious with my feelings. It was a heady blend of gratitude, shame, terror, and curiosity. But I never allowed myself to freak out or open up too much to anyone either. That would all happen down the road.

Two questions people often ask me about having both arms broken at the same time are, "How did you wipe your ass?" and "How did you masturbate?" Well, the first few times I did either were very painful. Since both of my arms had required surgery, the surgeon did them one at a time, allowing the first one to heal before taking away most of the use of the other one. But for details, on the ass wiping I would just wipe slowly and carefully and wince and moan as I did it. For the ball drainage (because that's basically what it was) I would just wait until I absolutely had to masturbate, like every week and a half, and then barricade myself in the bathroom, sit on the floor with my back against the door, so no one could come in (because I couldn't move quickly enough to leap up and yell, "I'm not masturbating!" as one occasionally has to do in normal life), then carefully take the brace off whichever arm was furthest from a surgery using my teeth and the fingertips of my other, casted arm, then I would slowly and tenderly masturbate. I'm actually nostalgic for those times, since it's so different from the way I assault myself now that I'm healthy.

But you're not the only people who are curious about how I masturbated in rehab with two broken arms. Oh, no! There was one meth addict at the hospital that was really curious about how I masturbated. Kelly was in rehab because her husband had found pictures of her sucking her meth dealer's dick. So he suggested she go to rehab while he took care of their daughter.

One night she had a girlfriend visit from the "real world." While sitting around with a group of people, Kelly said, "Hey, Rob, it must be hard to jerk off with your arms broken. My friend Lisa here will suck your dick if you want." Her friend Lisa nodded meekly and smiled. I declined and shuffled away as fast as I could, which was very slowly.

I was shocked when I later found out that people often fuck at rehab. It makes sense if you think about it, since the people there are all exploding disasters, but I think for me, I'd come as close to death as I saw fit and I really wanted to get better. I figured that putting my dick in the mouth of a crazy stranger was a blow job in the wrong direction. The more I think about it, the more I feel that that was the precise moment that I started to heal.

———

After exactly twenty-eight days at the hospital it was time to move on to a sober-living halfway house in West L.A. While rehab had been coed, the halfway house was one hundred percent dudes. It was kind of like sleepover camp.

While everyone in rehab was just totally broken, me included, people at the halfway house were a little further down the road to recovery; really taking a stab at actually living life without booze or drugs. The day I moved in, I was assigned a "big brother," Byron, who showed me around the place and told me the deal. He had brown teeth from smoking cocaine for ten years contrasted with probably the most beautiful blue eyes I've ever seen. He pointed out which bed would be mine and told me that since it was a bottom bunk I could hang a sheet from the top bed and make it into my own little "jack shack." A true big brother.

My roommates were a cute, chubby Armenian junkie from Glendale named Paul and an aggressive, muscular crackhead named Rick who terrified me. The first thing Rick said when I moved in and lay down on my bunk was, "Hey, wanna see where I got shot?" I said yes because I was afraid to say no, and he immediately pulled his pants down, spread his butt cheeks, and stuck his asshole right in my face. He then asked me if he could fuck my armpit on his birthday, which was coming up, because in prison, that's what his cellmate let him do. I was so scared I almost blacked out. Even if I was in my top physical shape, he could have killed me with his bare hands, and in my current condition I was absolutely defenseless with my arms in their casts.

Looking back, moments like that may help explain why I'm a comedian now. I could ONLY defend myself with humor. As hellish as all that sounds, Rick and I eventually became friends. He had an adorable wife and daughter who would visit him on weekends. When he wound up getting kicked out of the house for relapsing, I cried.

We got a third roommate after a while, a very wealthy crackhead who took the bunk above mine. He shook for days as he detoxed and my bed would essentially vibrate through the night. After he stabilized a bit he would regale us with stories of his opulent lifestyle paying hookers to watch him masturbate to porn.

We ate breakfast and dinner at the house as a group and had two weekly group meetings at the house. Thursday nights, a psychologist would come in to lead a discussion meeting with us, let's call her Elaine. She was crazier than most of the people in the house. One emblematic exchange with her went like this: Paul, a resident at the house, said at one meeting, "You know, I just would sit there and cut myself on the chest with a razor because I just, I felt that I deserved it . . . ."

Myrna yelled, "YES! I am the same way. I used to get so depressed I wouldn't make my bed. I would sleep on a bed WITH NO SHEETS!"

And then everybody would be totally nonplussed and we'd exchange glances suggesting, *"Hey, at least we're not as crazy as her,"* and then we'd pray for the ninety-minute meeting to end. It's kind that she volunteered her time to help people, but even twelve years later I look back at her and think: *BANANAS.*

The owner of the house was bonkers too, but in a good way. He was a black-clad biker with a big gray goatee and gruff voice he'd use to call us "bitches." His mind was utterly fried from drugs, but he just wanted to do what he could to help people get and stay clean. He was like a blue-collar angel; just a good guy in the trenches of life, getting dirty helping people. He provided people with a place to stay and started them on the path to getting better. And it worked for a lot of people. Not everyone, though.

Although I was only required by the judge to do one month in the halfway house, I wound up staying for almost four. I was too physically fucked up to work, so it was good to live with other people whose arms worked. And frankly, it was fun. It was a good group of guys and it felt great to be around them. They were, generally, taking a massive step forward in their lives, whether or not it would necessarily stick, and it felt good to live in a house that was charged with that energy. It created an atmosphere that was ripe for deep discussions and a lot of laughter.

It wasn't rare for someone to drift off during a conversation and say, "Holy shit. I can't believe I'm alive." Toward the end of my stay there, a frail little junkie moved in, and on his first day there, I asked him if he wanted to see where I got shot. He said yes, and I showed him. The circle was complete.

When I left the halfway house, I had one arm that totally worked and only a tiny cast on the other. I looked pretty much like a regular person and I felt reasonably ready to live on my own. I knew where to get help if I needed it, and for one shining moment I wasn't as afraid as I'd always been to appear vulnerable if I thought it might save my life. It was almost five months since the accident. A couple of guys from the house helped me move into my new apartment, which I planned to share with a friend from college.

Over the years I've done volunteer work in various rehabs and hospitals in the area. I've seen some guys from the house who've relapsed and wound up back where we started, or often in even worse shape. Rare is the second or third hospitalization for booze or drugs that's less disgusting than the first. While I hate seeing guys in that situation, it sure as shit drives home the severity of the issue. And only a small percentage of the people I've met in rehabs and hospitals since will remain sober. And though I can't identify them by sight or smell and wouldn't dare bet on who will succeed or fail in their sobriety, I like to be in the same room as them. I like to soak up their energy. It's a two-way street too, since I can tell them what worked for me in my efforts to keep the plug in the jug and trudge toward some measure of happiness and peace. But if I'm being honest (and fuck if that isn't Ingredient Number One in staying sober), I want to be around broken people who have just made the seismically powerful decision to get fixed. I want to feel their energy move throughout the hospital's ugly beige multipurpose room and let it wash over me. It gets me high.

rette. #cool @robdelaney. Child actors cry so realistically because their parents have given them a bottomless well of sadness to draw from. And... ACTION! @robdelaney On the 1st episode of Casper the Friendly Ghost, Casper the Friendly Boy was eaten by a clown behind his grandparents' barn. @robdelaney He'd come off way less pretentious if he went by Daniel "Dave" Lewis. @robdelaney My wife does a HILARIOUS John Goodman impression. Doesn't hurt that she looks exactly like him. @robdelaney I bet if Jeff Bridges picked up your kid from school today & said "I'm your dad now," your kid wouldn't even question it.

PART III   *la réhabilitation*

@robdelaney Can't live without your coffee? Tweet about it! @robdelaney GUY FIERI: "Just saying, I'm open all week if anybody requests me." MAKE-A-WISH FOUNDATION OPERATOR: "Stop fucking calling." @robdelaney. My freshman year of college I farted in a tiny crowded dorm room & a girl's younger sister who was visiting & wasn't even drunk threw up. @robdelaney A website that automatically plays music or needs to "load" is as outdated & terrible as slavery. @robdelaney I get anxious when there aren't at least 24 pieces of advertising within my field of vision. @robdelaney It's perfectly fine to offer raisins to a guest (if nuclear winter is upon us & you're living in an underground bunker) @robdelaney You know it's true love when your wife farts in bed & you go in the other room & text your boyfriend "I love you." @robdelaney @lancearmstrong I cheated on a vocab test in 9th grade, so I feel you brother. Ours is a lonely path. #strength @robdelaney Starbucks bathrooms are EXCLUSIVELY for terrible diarrhea, right? @robdelaney My children annoy me so I'm leaving everything in my will to a nap I took in 2007. @robdelaney I've never been to Japan, but I've seen a bunch of emojis so I think I get the idea. @robdelaney Watching real love on shows like The Bachelor makes me realize my own marriage is a fake bucket of shit. @robdelaney "I might be a sex virgin but I'm not a virgin at AWESOME MAGIC TRICKS!" *trips on cape, knocks over table with punchbowl & cookies* @robdelaney There should be a terrible show about a woman, her mom, and her daughter, all 3 named Jennifer, called "Jenerations" on Lifetime or the CW. @robdelaney Despite tensions between US & Russia, Putin offers to adopt Kim & Kanye's baby so that it may have a chance at "a normal life." @robdelaney GARY: "You wanna?" BARRY: "Ugh. Jesus OK." (Siamese twins deciding to masturbate) @robdelaney My son claims he "loves me," but the contents with

mes amis morts

Three guys died when I was at the halfway house: Chris, Arturo, and Luke. They all died right after I left in pretty quick succession. Each one hurt like a motherfucker.

I haven't been to war, so I can't comment on what that experience is like, but people who go through rehab or a halfway house walk a tough road together and not all of them make it. We knew we faced a powerful adversary that demanded respect. Unlike combat, the adversary was inside of us.

People die all kinds of ways from booze and drugs and they do it all the time. Funny, the other day I read the citations of several Army Rangers who were awarded the Silver Star for their actions in Afghanistan. It was beautiful stuff about beautiful young guys defending their brothers and sisters. Half of the citations were awarded to Rangers who rescued wounded men under heavy fire. My stepfather, Larry, was awarded the Silver Star for his heroics in Vietnam. He defended his men, got shot, and had to kill a lot of North Vietnamese soldiers to keep more of his guys from dying. Many, many died anyway. Larry has always been very respectful and supportive of my decision to get sober and recognized all the "legwork" I put into it. He's also been kind and sensitive about the depression I dealt with after I was in recovery. In no way am I comparing what I went through to what he went through; it's just that: a) I just recently read those brave Rangers' citations, and b) I am about to talk about the friends of mine who died while we were all in pursuit of the same goal. They're not heroes. And I'm me, so I know I'm not a hero. A memory surfaced today from my senior year of college in which I not infrequently masturbated to the woman who lived across Third Avenue from me in a big apartment building. She walked around nude, so it's not like I'm some sort of monster. Plus I had binoculars, so when in Rome . . . While you may not disagree with my decision to masturbate in the shadows while she, well within her rights, walked around her home nude, you can say with confidence that those aren't the actions of a hero. A hero would figure out which apartment she lived in, go ring her doorbell, and ask permission to masturbate openly while she folded laundry in the nude. That shows respect, discipline, and the hallmark of a real hero: courage. All of which I rarely display, especially when

I'm holding a boner in my hand. (It's my boner, by the way; I've never touched another man's erect penis. But I'm young yet.)

Chris was the first of my friends to die. He was a "rock star" and had been in a band whose videos I'd watched on MTV in the '80s. He was the prototypical rock dude; tall, incredibly skinny, with long dark hair and puffy bangs. He wore boots, tight jeans, sleeveless shirts, and the jangly bangles that guys in bands like to wear, for some reason. When he checked into the halfway house, he had a big abscess on his arm from where he'd gotten infected shooting up speedballs. Speedballs! Coke and heroin shot into your arm—the shit that killed John Belushi. I am laughing thinking about it; who in the fuck does that unless they are closing out all accounts and are fully one hundred percent at peace with dying at ANY moment?

What's funny to me is that I never really did drugs. I smoked a lot of pot, but I'm among those who think that doesn't really count. Not that it can't make your life shitty and boring and a little shorter due to pizza overindulgence and general malaise, but there are certainly plenty of perfectly well-adjusted people who smoke a doob now and then and suffer, roughly, no negative consequences. I'd take "pills" if they were handed out, and I took acid once and did mushrooms and smoked opium a few times. But that's it. I never did coke or heroin. And meth showed up after my substance abuse had been sort of "codified," so that just didn't seem like something to explore. I believed, as I was told growing up, that crack was indeed whack, so that never called out to me. And I guess it's a little surprising that I never did coke if you look at the big picture, but I have an explanation for that. In 1986, the Boston Celtics drafted twenty-two-year-old Len Bias, a preternaturally gifted forward from the University of Maryland. I was nine. Right before he was supposed to join the team for training, he did some coke at a party, immediately had a heart attack, and fucking died. It was the first time I'd heard of cocaine and it was introduced to me as something that killed beautiful athletes. His death rocked Boston and all Celtics fans. So COCAINE WILL KILL YOU IF YOU TRY IT EVEN ONCE was permanently imprinted on me.

Once, in college, my friend Michael and I were blind drunk on a bench in Union Square talking about Len Bias's death, which was still fresh in our memories, and we made a pledge that we would never do cocaine and if either of us were thinking about it, we could call the other for a talk-down off the ledge of certain death. So even when I was an abject alcoholic scumbag, years deep into my booze problem, riding the subway IN THE MORNING with visibly urine-soaked pants, I remained terrified of coke.

Plus, I liked to go "down" with things that I ingested, not "up." I wanted to ride the wave, not explode, or go *pop pop pop*, or talk a lot, like coke seemed to make people do. Instead, I drank my beer and wine and bourbon and loved it. Even though my drinking could have landed me in the same cemetery as a crack smoker who got shot in an argument over money, I did and do view hard drug use as exotic and effectively forbidding.

It's a weird little "moral" code. I put "moral" in quotation marks because it has nothing to do with morals but it was a sort of guiding prejudice that guided how I thought back then: "drugs = bad; drinking = fine." But as we know, booze kills more people than every other drug combined and then multiplied. By what number I don't know. Let's go with thirteen, though it's probably more. Eighty-six? Probably too high. Look, this isn't a math book, and I'm tired of you yelling numbers at me.

Chris, despite his rock-star looks, was quite down to earth and fun to be around. I got a charge out of talking to someone that "cool." He would have correspondingly "rock"-y chicks visit him at the halfway house. They had dyed blond hair, tight outfits, and big fake boobs. It's funny how birds of a feather do in fact flock together and, in the case of rock-and-roll people, many of them do really look like birds, with their plumage and their struts. And their silicone tits. (All birds have silicone tits; look it up.)

Chris was a fixture at our nightly visits to get frozen yogurt. Most nights, a gang of us would go and occupy a corner of a little frozen shop in West L.A. You'd have guys just out of jail, actual rock stars, guys who'd been living on the street, and tall, gangly me in my two casts. Every night I'd get chocolate and vanilla swirled in a cup with crumbled Heath bar on top. My urge to eat sweets in the months after quitting drinking was INSANE. A lot of other people I've spoken to have said the same thing; they developed a crazy sweet tooth in early sobriety. Maybe the dopamine hit you get from sugar approximated a weak high? Whatever the case, I ate the fuck out of some frozen yogurt with Heath on top.

A girl named Mindy worked behind the counter at Yogurt Town. She was adorable and had blond hair and dark brown eyes. Since I looked like a medical curiosity, I didn't flirt or anything; I just tried to be Mr. Polite Nice Guy and I was very happy when she rewarded me with a smile. Where are you now, Mindy? Maybe she works in the Department of Health and Human Services in Washington and is pregnant with her second child. Maybe she's caring for her mother who has multiple sclerosis and is writing a book much, much better than this one. Maybe she still works at Yogurt Town because it works well with her PhD program at UCLA. Maybe she was a hallucination that my brain chose to show me night after night because it knew I could use a bright spot as I navigated the medical and legal labyrinths of my first year off booze.

I don't remember what Chris would order at Yogurt Town, but we probably went there ten times together. Then I left the halfway house, and a short while later he shot up the speedball that killed him. The last time I'd spoken to him he was excited about some session work he was going to do with David Bowie.

The second friend to die was Arturo. He was a short Mexican bass player from Austin. I liked him right away because he had a Danzig tattoo. Anybody who felt strongly enough about the bands of Glenn Danzig to emblazon his weird goat/devil skull on his shoulder was A-OK in my book. The house took in a lot of guys from Austin since it had a relationship with Musi-

Cares and the Musicians' Assistance Program—two groups that helped musicians get sober. Austin has lots of musicians and musicians get high sometimes.

Arturo was just a little cutie pie, really. He reminded me a bit of my childhood friend Todd, a kid who liked to play music, have fun, and just generally be warm and pleasant and fun to be around, but Arturo was also a crack smoker. One day Arturo came to me with a quandary. He told me that he'd met a guy at a mental health facility where he attended group therapy. The guy invited him to his house after therapy one time, and Arturo went. They hung out a bit and the guy showed him some records and gave him a soda or something. Then he asked Arturo if he'd like to jerk off with him. "No touching each other or anything; we'll just jerk off together. Just a couple of dudes jerking off. No big deal." Arturo declined and later that day he asked me what I thought. He said, "I don't know—is it rude that I told him no? He's a nice guy and everything. Do guys jerk off together and I just don't know that? I don't do it with my friends in Austin. Do you jerk off with your guy friends?"

I wanted to cry. What a little snuggle muffin he was! He was really young and despite drug addiction hadn't been out in the world enough or seen enough good behavior modeled to know that it is a major-league-wacky anomaly for straight dudes to take out their dongs and play with them together even if they don't touch. I told him that I personally reserved masturbation for "me time" or for the confines of a romantic relationship. Other than that, jerking off was off the table for social situations. I told him that was nonnegotiable and that even if he,

Arturo, and I were friends for years to come, he could rest assured that I would never ever ask him to jerk off with and/or near me. I told him that the dude who asked him was a nutjob and as "nice" as he might be in other areas, it was a very, very awful idea to jerk off with someone you've just met at a group therapy meeting at a hospital.

In addition to eating a lot of sugary foods in early sobriety, it can also be tempting to jerk off all the time. The desire for human comfort and closeness can be acute. A hug is like Christmas—or at least it was for me. Some people don't want to be touched at all, I'm sure. Whatever your wants and perceived needs are at that stage, you are nothing if not raw. So a young kid from out of town, giving up his crutch of drugs, would be very vulnerable to a "kind" stranger and would and should be forgiven for wondering, *"Should I jerk off with this guy?"* You don't know. He didn't know. He was lonely and fucked up and learning how to live.

I don't know what happened when Arturo left the house and went back to Austin, but it wasn't good, because a few weeks later we got word that he'd shot himself. I don't know what to say beyond that. I don't know if he got high and did it or if the prospect of living without getting high was so unappealing that he didn't want to live at all. And I never will know. But I know that he was a good guy and I enjoyed the couple of months I got to spend with him.

The third friend who died was Luke. Luke was an emergency room doctor. He was also one of the most handsome guys I've ever seen. He was muscular and blond and blue-eyed. He looked like Captain Mister Doctor Nordic America. It'd be tempting to hate a guy like that on sight, but he was nice, too. He helped me interpret my intake paperwork from when I was admitted to the emergency room after my accident. When you get admitted to an emergency room with a bunch of problems and they have to do a bunch of procedures with cops present, a fair amount of paperwork is generated. I had a big packet of stuff along with the police report that I would thumb through occasionally in an effort to piece together exactly what had happened.

It was all fairly self-explanatory, but there was one anatomical phrase that I didn't understand. It said, "There is no blood present at the meatus." I'd never seen the word "meatus." It sounded very terribly disgusting and I gathered it was good that there was no blood "present" at it. This was pre-smartphones and whenever I'd meant to look it up, there wasn't a dictionary around so I just had to remain curious about it and let the query sink back into my subconscious the way we all used to do.

Anyway, after Luke and I had been shooting the breeze about various emergency room shenanigans he'd seen, I remembered to ask him what a meatus was, and he told me it was the opening of the urethra at the tip of the penis. Or the vagina. What a fucking awful word. It has "meat" in it but then it's pronounced as a three-syllable word with two for "meat," so "mee-ay-tus." Yuck. It's a strong candidate for my least favorite word. It's as gross as calling it a "penis meat-hole." If there are any doctors reading this, please band together and push to just have it called a penis meat-hole. Don't pull any punches.

Luke was at a halfway house because he'd become addicted to Oxycontin. It's generally accepted that doctors as a population have a higher percentage of addicts than non-doctors. And when they have ready access to drugs as delightful as Oxycontin and other synthetic opiates, it's easy to imagine them indulging. Though I'd never taken them before I got sober, I was prescribed Vicodin and was given Dilaudid at the hospital and those drugs felt utterly wonderful coursing through my veins. You don't just feel like you're wrapped in a blanket; you feel like you *are* a beautiful blanket, being blown around the Caribbean, high in the sky. If I didn't think they'd set me on a path that would end pretty quickly at the morgue, I'd take a few right now. But therein lies the rub; you feel too good when you take them. The way synthetic opiate painkillers work is that they don't remove the pain; they make you not care that you're experiencing pain. Your arm or head or whatever's been injured might still throb, but you note the "pain" and think, *"Throb away, lil' buddy, I am too busy doing lazy somersaults through the ether with Jesus."* So they're incredibly dangerous.

Luke had a girlfriend who would come by the house and play guitar and sing with a sexy, smoky voice. I liked her and would have thoughts like, *"I wish they weren't together and that my arms worked so that maybe she would go out with me."* Since I liked both of them, though, I just admired her from afar.

Shortly after I left the house and moved in with my friend

Ali from college, I got a call from one of the guys and he told me that Luke had OD'd and died. I was crushed. He was a doctor and so fucking handsome and smart and nice. Shouldn't all that have added up into some sort of cosmic or karmic armor that protected him? What was his fucking SAT score? His death was more of a shock than Chris's because I figured Luke was just lured by his easy access to prescription meds and that he would get it together after getting burned. How were people like me supposed to stay sober if handsome doctors could just up and relapse and die?

A few days later his brother called me. I'd never met his brother, but he'd gotten phone numbers of some of the guys Luke had told him about and decided to call them. He cried as he spoke to me and I'm crying right now thinking about it. He asked me to stay sober because he didn't want anybody else to die like his brother did. He loved his brother and he called me, a stranger, to ask me to not get loaded again and die, to honor his brother. I don't know about the value of blood pacts or oaths, but I know that when I recall that conversation, with me sitting on the edge of my bed, stunned and crying, listening to another man cry, I am prompted to stay the fuck sober and try to help others do the same.

Naturally, in the years since, other people I met in the early days have died, but those three guys all died within weeks of one another, immediately after I'd left the house. It was like the grim reaper swooped through my pals, cutting them down, saying, "Fuck you clowns. You think this is a joke? This is it. Pick up a bottle. Pick up a bottle and see what happens." I think of Chris, Arturo, and Luke a lot. I really feel them in me, sort of seated in my heart and along for the ride. I feel stronger when I think about them too. I cry, of course, but they're not just cautionary tales to me; they're not excuses to say, "There but for the grace of God go I," they're my friends and I sort of think of it like we're on the path together. They may have vacated their earthly bodies, but they're welcome to ride in my hairy, borrowed vessel to reach the goal, whatever it may be. And I don't know what it is, but I do feel compelled to do what Luke's brother asked of me, and I'm grateful for the opportunity. I imagine miniature versions of them, in my pockets, shooting the breeze as I walk into the Yogurt Town to get us all frozen yogurt.

dépression!

After three and a half months in the halfway house, I moved in with my friend Ali. We'd met at NYU and then reconnected after we'd both moved to L.A. She was a busy editor and had a boyfriend and wasn't really around much. I was busy returning to normal life and picking up jobs doing catering and temping. After living with her for not quite six months, she decided she wanted to get her own place, so I was charged with finding myself another roommate. The first sign that something was off was my reaction to her telling me she was moving out. I remember being disproportionately upset at the news.

She didn't present it as some horrible bombshell, and she

had no reason to. She had a boyfriend and was tired of living in a small apartment in Koreatown and wanted to get a house.

And I didn't do or say anything other than, "Okay, good luck!" but inside I was terrified.

Rather than thinking, *"C'est la vie, another chapter in the journey that is life"* . . . I was devastated.

It wasn't that we had any kind of special relationship—we'd never dated or hooked up or anything like that, nor was our friendship ending, just our cohabitation—but I remember thinking, *"How will I possibly find another roommate or place to live? How could anyone do that? It's impossible."* What should have seemed like a quotidian, normal "hiccup" really, seemed an insurmountable problem. That was really the first clue that something was wrong. Up to that moment in life, absent booze, I'd met with life's vicissitudes in a pretty average to good manner. But now I was frantic. At the time, I was going to a psychologist every other Tuesday to just talk stuff out. My "big brother" at the halfway house had suggested that talking to a therapist would be a good idea due to the overtly, comically self-destructive nature of some of the things I did when I was drunk, like climbing telephone poles, jumping down onto subway tracks, and driving into buildings. I'd found therapy very useful and I enjoyed going. It just felt good to get in the regular habit of telling somebody the truth about how I felt. Whether you're in a good mood or a bad mood, I can't imagine hashing out your issues with a disinterested professional third party would ever be a bad idea.

In addition to the terrible fear of Ali moving out and what

that would mean for me, I started to not be able to sleep at night. I didn't tell Ali about this because I was at least aware of the fact that my feelings didn't really have anything to do with her. Perhaps I was just afraid to be by myself. After a couple of weeks, she moved out, and I started to get more depressed. I was temping some days and hating it, tiptoeing around offices, terrified of making a mistake or standing out or even having to talk to anyone. I would fall asleep when I went to bed at night, but I'd wake up pretty soon after and then not be able to go back to sleep. I was just gripped by terror. I began to think about suicide. The nights would be awful, and then when I woke up, I'd have terrible diarrhea, since my churning stomach liquefied anything that went into it, which, after a while, wasn't much. When I'd brush my teeth in the morning, the act of touching the toothbrush to my tongue would make me vomit. Every single day. Brushing my teeth would fill me with dread. I lost all sexual desire too. My libido had always been probably average or leaning slightly toward high, but it just totally evaporated. I wasn't seeing anyone at the time, so this just meant I didn't masturbate anymore. I began to express my concerns to family and a couple of people I'd met at the halfway house. They were all kind to me but I felt like I was talking to them through a thick cement wall.

Evaluating my life circumstances made me think, *"I should probably wrap this up."* I would constantly envision blowing my head apart with a shotgun blast or swimming out into the ocean until I got tired and drowned.

I wasn't secretive about feeling low, but I was afraid to fully unfurl the horror of what I was imagining for my family and close friends to see. My therapist said that she'd like me to see a psychiatrist to look at the possibility of going on medication for depression. I resisted for a few weeks, for all the normal reasons someone might; I thought it would be "weak" and that I should "soldier through." But part of me, a very tiny part, recognized that something was very wrong. I'd quit drinking and drugs. I'd surrounded myself with good healthy people who were doing the same. I was eating healthy. I was exercising. I was going to therapy and genuinely striving to live my life in a kind manner. I wasn't harboring any secrets that were weighing me down. In essence, I was doing everything one could reasonably expect me to do to "feel good." But I didn't feel good at all. I didn't sleep. I shit only fiery liquid. Brushing my teeth made me puke. My whole body ached. My particular depression was accompanied by intense physical pain. I ached all over, all the time. I had no sexual desire of any kind. And mind you, I'd masturbated days after the accident with two broken arms and regularly while living in rehab and in the halfway house. During those times, I'd actually been delighted that THAT desire hadn't deserted me. But it sure as shit was gone now, along with even the slightest positive thought or belief. I saw doom everywhere, especially when my eyes were closed.

Another bizarre aspect of my depression was the obsessive-compulsive behavior that attended it. I involuntarily kept my hands balled into fists, squeezing my thumb the way a newborn does. Time and again I'd look down and realize they'd squeezed up again and force myself to relax them. Also, whenever I parked my car somewhere, I'd get out and walk toward my destination, then be seized by the fear that I hadn't locked my car. Sometimes I'd get a few blocks away and then have to return to the car to be sure I'd locked it. This was doubly odd because it was a sixteen-year-old Volvo station wagon that no one would have stolen if I'd left it unlocked and running. Plus its contents were McDonald's wrappers and apple cores and Fugazi cassettes, so no one would even want to break in. But fuck me if I was going to leave that treasure on wheels unlocked. It was so odd and unsettling. I'd park, walk toward whatever shitty purgatorial experience I had in store, then the thought *"DID YOU LOCK YOUR CAR?"* would thunder through my brain and not shut up until I'd gone back and verified that, JUST LIKE EVERY OTHER FUCKING TIME I'd acquiesced to the voice, my car was indeed locked.

Twice in a short period of time I drove away from a gas station, leaving the cap to my gas tank behind. Studies have shown that people who suffer from depression are more likely to experience dementia when they're elderly, and I don't doubt that for a second. You get a little preview—a teaser, if you will—of what that nightmare must be like with depression. Dementia would certainly ride well on the thought grooves established by depression. I'm certainly not resigned to dementia; fuck that. I read, exercise, write, and try to keep my mind malleable and in good shape. Plus it would be terribly silly to hear about a study that posited a negative future for yourself and then believe it.

There is massive, pulsing truth in the statement "Ignorance is bliss." Willful ignorance or resistance to alleged facts has been a big ingredient in any success I've had.

"Ride it out," I would tell myself every night. *"Don't do anything. You can always kill yourself tomorrow."* I'd try to push that thought away every day. After weeks of abject horror, I thought, *"I will try medication, and if that doesn't help, then I can kill myself."* I thought about my friends from the halfway house who'd overdosed or committed suicide in the past few months and wondered if I was destined to join them. I finally relented, after talking to my therapist and several relatives who came forward and told me they'd benefited from medication. I decided to give it a shot.

I remember saying goodbye to my sister, over the phone, as she was preparing to spend a semester of her junior year in Spain. This was when I was at my absolute lowest and about to fold and take medication. I tried to steel myself as we spoke and not give away how depressed and scared I was. I was afraid that I might do something to myself and would never see her again. My beautiful little sister, my best friend. She's five years younger than me, so between that and the fact that we're opposite sexes, we were never competitive about anything and were just free to be pals pretty much from the day she was born. I remember being in fifth grade and seeing her come around a corner one day as a kindergartner and just being ecstatic to see her, even though I'd seen her at home three hours earlier and would see her there again three hours later. It's pretty much the same when I see her now. Although I do remember trying to teach her how to wash dishes when we were little and her taking two infuriating hours to do it because she refused to run the water above a tiny trickle. Other than that, she's a good person.

After our parents' divorce, which happened when she was nine and I was fourteen, we became very close and assumed larger roles in each other's lives as our parents dropped a few rungs from infallible god people to flawed earthlings.

Funny. As I think about that phone call now, it's actually almost a fond memory, because it represented an actual feeling—sadness—and I hadn't felt anything in what felt like an eternity. I think it's important to explain that major depression is not even peripherally related to "sadness." Depression is the absence of emotion. I never cried during my darkest periods of depression. Crying would have been A HOLIDAY. It would have been FUCKING CHRISTMAS. A fight or a feeling of anger would have been AN EASTER EGG HUNT AT DISNEYLAND. I am vocal about my depression now because it was so fucking Satanically awful that I view it as one of my life's primary missions to help other people understand and overcome it.

Depression kills people because in the normal weather patterns of human emotion over a day or a week or a decade, actual unipolar major depressive disorder doesn't appear. It's like The Nothing in *The NeverEnding Story*. It eats your anger, your sadness, your happiness, your testicles and/or ovaries. Your solid shit. And it would love to kill you dead and attend your funeral and call your mother a cunt as you're lowered into the ground after a closed-casket funeral where everyone was mad at you. What's funny is how much less afraid I am now of anything life throws at me.

Another good way to illustrate how bad it is, is to say that it made being in jail in a wheelchair with four broken limbs feel like a cruise among the Greek Isles. (I've never been to the Greek Isles, but that's the first lovely thing that sprang to my currently nondepressed mind.) I might also add that while depressed, creativity or imagination is close to impossible. Those who think that depression is "good" for creative people may form a line and very aggressively blow me. I may be "creative" or a "weirdo" but I'm one thousand [literally] times more productive and useful to my fellow man when I'm firing on all happy cylinders. Just to be clear, I'd rather be in jail than depressed in my apartment. A jail sentence ends. You know roughly when it will end too. I would rather have four broken limbs in jail than be depressed and fully ambulatory and independent. Broken bones knit and wounds heal. There is a commonly agreed upon method for fixing them too; you set them or stitch them up. Properly and thoroughly treating depression is much touchier. There are numerous types of medication and therapies and any honest doctor will tell you that trying to fix it involves rolling the dice, or, as they might call it, "trial and error." What a horrible term.

I am very, very ecstatically happy to report that the first medication my psychiatrist prescribed, worked. For the record, it was Lexapro, a selective serotonin reuptake inhibitor. I remember sitting on his couch, sullen, emaciated, and folded in on myself, with dark circles under my eyes, wondering, *"Can this Russian psychiatrist help me?"* (Since the information flow in his office was primarily a one-way street from me to him, the only things I knew about him were that he was Russian, he had two kids, and he saw patients only one day a week. The other days he worked in the Los Angeles jail system.) He gave me a sample packet of Lexapro and a prescription. I left his office and drove to a pharmacy and bought a pill cutter because the first week I was only supposed to take half a pill. I remember sitting in my car and cutting the first pill and it shot out of the pill cutter and landed somewhere on the floor of my car. I panicked. Even though I had a full prescription, I literally thought that the pills were little puzzle pieces that might add up to sanity for me, so the possibility of losing one half of one pill would be a travesty that couldn't be remedied. I found it under my seat after scouring my car's dirty floor and put it in my mouth.

That evening I felt an inkling of peace, not because the chemicals had begun to work, but because I felt I'd surrendered to the fact that other people cared about me and might have a better idea about what I should do to get better and because going to a psychiatrist, getting a prescription, and filling it was a tacit admission that even I believed (somewhere in my addled mind) that I deserved to feel better.

Gradually, I did begin to feel better. After a while I could brush my teeth without vomiting. My poops began to firm up and exit my butt as horrible solids rather than horrible liquid. After a couple of weeks, I noticed a familiar *feistiness* in my trousers, and when I addressed it, the amount of semen I produced was around seven hundred gallons. (I'm estimating.) Most wonderful of all though: I could sleep again. I didn't wake up at 11:15 after having been asleep for forty-five minutes and lie in bed terrified for seven hours. I began to interact with other people more at work and socially. I asked women on dates and sometimes they said yes. Only a couple of months later, I did my first stand-up open mic.

which he fills diapers he KNOWS I'LL BE CHANG-ING suggests otherwise. **@robdelaney Why do babies have to cry? Why couldn't they like, glow, or beep rhythmically to get our attention? Shitty babies...** @robdelaney "I saw a really nice chair yesterday." - if your grandma tweeted **@robdelaney Just bought diapers and toilet paper because all my family does is shit.** @robdelaney I hope there's a magazine for cool college bros called "Frattitude." **@robdelaney Obviously we have our own shitty lives to worry about now but it would be fun to all move into a Twitter nursing home in 50 years.** @robdelaney If you use the term "man card" seri-

PART IV *la romance*

ously, I assume you use it to access your "man cave," so you can hunker down & gobble some "man dong." **@robdelaney Hey, if the mood's right under the mistletoe, don't be afraid to go in for a little mistlefinger.** @robdelaney Look at your disgusting balls. That's LITERALLY exactly what Jesus wants them to look like. #Bible **@robdelaney Not much of a "First Aid" kit if it doesn't have peanut butter in it.** @robdelaney Listen up: I wear the pants in this family. They're a lovely taffeta with a subtle flare to draw attention to my lace-up sandals. **@robdelaney Drive-thru worker just re-**

coiled in horror when I rolled down my window & she got walloped by a bucket of moist farts. @robdelaney You know you're getting old when you forget the name of the street you grew up on and break your hip and die. @robdelaney @Garfield because of your "cartoon" I fed my beloved Mr. Turtle lasagna & coffee for his birthday & he died. I will fuck your soul. @robdelaney Just thought I caught my wife looking at porn; turns out she was shopping for underwear for herself. What a fucking pervert. @robdelaney Bittersweet: Got the very last DustBuster at @Walmart, but the old man I beat to death to get it was my wife in disguise. @robdelaney It is alleged that Guy Fieri was hiding in the turkey Obama pardoned & can thus never be prosecuted for war crimes. @robdelaney Don't even FRONT like you love your family, America, or God if you don't have a DETAILED & REHEARSED Black Friday tactical shopping plan. @robdelaney That awkward moment someone begins a tweet with "that awkward moment" & I slap their face with my dong. @robdelaney I just read a pamphlet about sex & I'm gonna be honest: it sounds pretty cool. @robdelaney "Hey man… my mouth is like… a zoo for teeth…" - Mitt Romney, wandering around the Utah desert on peyote, 11/8/2012 @robdelaney Remember when putting something on the internet was the equivalent of hiding it in a

SIDA?

I'd had close to no sex when I got to college. When I was seventeen, I lost my virginity to my girlfriend and she to me. The experience was "nice" and we drove around and smoked unfiltered Camels afterward. About a year later I got drunk at a party and had sex with a girl I didn't know terribly well on my friend's waterbed. I'm sure I was both flailing and unskilled, but I can at least tell today's teens that I had sex on a waterbed—something they'll never do since nobody buys waterbeds anymore because they're stupid. In other words, my penis had been inside a couple of girls, but I didn't really know what to do with it, and I could have been charitably described as "very awful" at sex.

When it came time for me to pick a college, I chose NYU. I'd decided I wanted to be an actor and NYU had a renowned musical theater program. I figured if I wanted to act, and do it well, why not train the hell out of my body and voice rather than just study scripts, frown, and pretend an empty glass was filled with orange juice. From what I understand, that's what one does in a regular acting class. I, on the other hand, wanted to sing and dance all day, every day—which is exactly what I did. During my college search, I only looked at schools in Boston and New York. As great as the schools in Boston were, I thought it would be more edifying to venture a little farther from home to a city I knew roughly nothing about. It proved to be a good decision, since merely living in New York City forced me to constantly vacuum up nonstop stimuli through every sensory door. Add college to that equation and you can see how it was a very thorough educational experience.

When I arrived at NYU, I made a concerted effort—as part of my well-rounded education—to get my dinky stinky as often as possible. I was AS A RULE drunk anytime I even kissed a girl my freshman year, and none of those sexual experiences stand out in my mind as anything other than clumsy and desperate. That said, I definitely got some fuckin' done.

Early in my first semester I wound up having drunken and somewhat athletic unprotected sex with a girl who was in about forty of my classes. I wanted to make sure we could relive the horror eleven or twelve times a day when we made unintentional eye contact. The awkwardness was compounded by the fact that we were firmly established pals before we got fucked-up and curdled our relationship with drunk sex. College!

A couple of days later I noticed some little red bumps peeking out among my pubic hair. I was eighteen and had begun puberty at that magic time in the 1980s when kids were taught that having unprotected sex even once meant you'd die of AIDS within six months, and then your mom would have to light a picture of your face on fire in front of the White House and disown your memory in a special ceremony. I was sincerely terrified and I figured the extreme fatigue I was feeling wasn't from my terrible hangover or from being up late studying, but rather from my rapidly diminishing T-cell count.

I was too ashamed and scared to talk to any friends or family, so all I could think to do was to go to NYU's health services and find out how fast-acting my particular strand of AIDS was. I sat in the waiting room imagining how, exactly, I would tell my mom I arrived at college and, as my first order of business, immediately went out and got AIDS. The doctor who saw me was an older gentleman who didn't seem shocked by my AIDS. In fact, he said pretty quickly that it didn't look like any STD he knew of. He thought it was probably just a heat rash or a skin irritation of some kind, but just to be safe, he suggested that I go to a dermatologist.

I walked a half a block to the dermatologist's office and sat in the waiting room, still figuring that I had some type of advanced AIDS rash which would perhaps take many forms before it finally appeared as Death bearing a scythe and a wheelbarrow to cart me off to the particular hell reserved for naughty eighteen-year-old boys who drink alcohol, do marijuana, and then put their penis in nice people. I was eventually sent to an examination room where a ravishingly beautiful young woman, not possibly over twenty-seven years old, walked in.

"Hello. How can we help you today?"

"Oh, Jesus."

"What's the matter?"

"Well, um, I really wish that you were an old man and not a young woman."

"Don't be silly; I have all sorts of patients. Young and old, male and female. No reason to be embarrassed about anything."

"Okay . . ."

"So you have a rash?"

"Yeah."

"Can I see it?"

I unzipped my pants and pulled down my boxers so that the top of my pubic hair was just visible.

"Take them all the way down."

I pulled my pants and underwear down, fully exposing my eighteen-year-old penis and testicles to an extraordinarily beautiful young doctor with long brown hair and green eyes who smelled very good.

She stuck her face right on in there and checked everything thoroughly. Then she said this to me: "Is there any irritation around your anus?"

"NO. NO, THERE IS NOT. MY ANUS IS FINE."

"How do you know? You can't see it. Let me take a quick look."

"I am certain there is no rash there."

"Turn around."

I turned around.

"Spread your buttocks open."

I peeled apart my fear-clamped butt cheeks and showed her my shameful little butthole. She leaned over in her chair and gazed into it. I prayed fervently that God would give me a fatal stroke.

"Looks okay to me. Nothing out of the ordinary back there. You can pull your pants up."

I pulled my pants up and she wrote out a prescription for a topical cream that she claimed should clear the rash right up. I ran from her Washington Square Park office.

Why, I asked myself, *WHY did she need to look at my butthole?* Couldn't she have prescribed the cream based on what she saw up front? Was she some type of butthole enthusiast? Should a doctor be allowed to be so beautiful? Was she really a doctor at all or had I been tricked and filmed by the *Candid Camera: Special Butthole Unit*? I was on fire with embarrassment and shame. I had spread open my most secret of areas and a beautiful woman I had just met had CAREFULLY STUDIED IT. She could draw my butthole from memory! Later that night, as she lay in bed replaying her day, she might think about my butthole. Over lunch, with another beautiful young doctor, she might say, "I saw the weirdest butthole today." Perhaps the girl

I'd had athletic sex with had been unsatisfied and hired an actress to dress up as a doctor and shame me. ALL THESE WERE POSSIBILITIES.

The third place I visited that day was a clinic where they drew a vial of my blood.

They sent me a letter a week later that said, "Congratulations! You do not have AIDS." I'm paraphrasing; I really should have saved it. It probably said something like "HIV STATUS: NEGATIVE" or something clinical and deliciously severe.

After my inaugural AIDS test at age eighteen, I became a diligent condom carrier and when most subsequent lovers had the good fortune to lie under my grunting, sweaty mass, they were always the grimacing recipient of an eager and rubber-sheathed penis boner.

une liaison fatale

I've eaten a lot of Zankou Chicken. Zankou Chicken is a chain of restaurants in Los Angeles that serve amazing Armenian fast food. I'd be more than content to have a chicken Tarna plate with their signature garlic paste for my last meal on Earth. If you can't eat there anytime soon, you can listen to Beck's brilliant soul epic, "Debra," in which it's featured. No one who's eaten at Zankou is surprised that Beck felt the need to immortalize the restaurant in a song. It's that good.

In 2003, four years after Beck wrote and released "Debra," Zankou Chicken's cancer-riddled owner, Mardiros Iskenderian, shot and killed his sister, his mother, and then himself, because he allegedly didn't trust his closest relatives to run the Zankou Empire after he died.

I had eaten at the Hollywood Zankou Chicken the night before, after one of my earliest stand-up experiences, where I told a joke about cartography that bombed so bad that Mr. Iskenderian would have been acquitted if he'd shot me, too.

Eight years later, Zankou Chicken had nine locations around Los Angeles and was running strong. One day I went to the West L.A. Zankou, since it happened to be located between a meeting I had and an audition for a role in a show about an invisible dog. I hadn't been to Zankou in a long time, so I was excited. Their proprietary blend of cinnamon, nutmeg, and garlic is as satisfying as a mid-grade sexual experience. It is genuinely exciting to eat their food; it's like your mouth is learning something as it chews.

I ordered a chicken Tarna plate and a medium Pepsi. They gave me a number and I found a table next to a window. As I sat down, I knocked over my Pepsi and its cap came off. The entire contents of the cup poured out onto my crotch. Twenty-four ounces of Pepsi soaked my jeans, its landfall centering on my penis and wreaking havoc outward.

The other Zankou patrons were happy. You can't blame them—it's fun to see someone spill things on himself, especially when the result is a wetness pattern that resembles nothing other than urine. A pretty Asian woman in an expensive business outfit handed me some napkins. I wasn't embarrassed. I was more fascinated by the spill's majesty, its perfection. It was a great spill, centered as it was on my crotch, and I did not have time to go home and change my pants before my audition, nor did I know where I could buy a new pair of pants in time. I was preparing to go to an audition with visibly wet pants and "see what happened."

I wasn't going to let soaking wet pants prevent me from eating my chicken Tarna, however, so I dug in and vacuumed up those succulent chicken chunks and mentally rehearsed for my meeting, saying things like "This? Oh, it's just urine," or "I like to take away any negotiating advantage you may have by pissing myself in advance. Now let's do this."

When I was done with my chicken and replacement Pepsi, I walked the two or three blocks back to my car, which was parked on the side of Sepulveda Boulevard. I noticed a commotion gathered near it. People were clustered in groups and half of them were looking up toward the top of a four-story parking garage across the street. When I reached my car, I saw that they were surveying a brand-new hole in the side of the building's top story. I then followed the gaze of the other half of the crowd down to the Mercedes SUV lying upside down in the middle of the intersection now filling with emergency personnel. The top of the car had been totally crushed. Instead of being about six feet tall, it was now only around three and a half feet tall.

A guy said to me, "An old lady drove through the wall. She's dead."

I didn't want to stick around while they pulled her out, so I got in my car and drove toward my meeting. I rolled down all my windows, opened my sunroof, and turned the air on full blast in an effort to dry my pants. It worked reasonably well. Only an astute observer would have noticed the faded brown rim that traced from the middle of one calf, up around my crotch, and back down to the other calf. No one said anything if they did notice.

I haven't been back to Zankou and I might never go again. I don't want any more people to have to die.

le beguin

I spent my junior year of college in Paris. I enjoyed French film and literature, and it seemed like Henry Miller had a good time there, so I thought I should go check it out. When I applied for NYU's Paris program, one question commanded more of my attention than the others: Would I prefer to live in my own apartment or in a French household? I figured living with a family would help with my language acquisition, so I picked "household." But when I arrived some months later, I was reminded that "household" doesn't have to mean "family." It can mean a big apartment inhabited by one eighty-five-year-old woman. And that's what it did mean, for me. I became roommates with a lovely old woman named Jacqueline who lived in the apartment where she was born in 1912, was raised, and survived Paris's Nazi occupation. And as one of her final earthly adventures, she got me as a roommate. While we didn't spend too much time together, when we did, she'd ask me to bring her pizza and, if it wasn't too much trouble, to put on my red sweater that she fancied. In retrospect, I admire her: having a strapping foreign student bring you pizza and dress by request? I think that might even be sex to an eighty-five-year-old. Ahh, Jacqueline, I miss you. You are one hundred and one now, and/or dead.

Most of the other American kids that were in my NYU program only signed up for a semester, but I figured one semester wouldn't really be long enough to get a good handle on the French language, so I, and a few other diehards, went for a full year. That proved to be a good decision because only at the very end of my first semester I realized, "Holy shit; I speak French." I'd taken French back in eighth and ninth grade, then met with a tutor a few times in the weeks leading up to my departure, so it is encouraging to know that brutal immersion into a country that speaks another language can result in language proficiency, even in adulthood.

The kids who went for the full year were, as a rule, bonkers. There was a German basketball player who was six foot six and had long, black hair; a brilliant former child model who, a few years after we left, returned to France to marry a billionaire imam and literally became a princess; and a kind and hilarious bookworm junkie with whom I remain friends to this day, both of us having gotten sober twelve years ago, only days apart. So the people who went for the full year represented a great crew. They were all too smart for their own good, and they loved to get fucked up, just like me.

During my second semester, I took a class in art history that was taught by a tall, thin, green-eyed woman named Madame Royer. I had a crush on her and would dream about her frequently. She also happened to live right next to our school with her husband and two beautiful children. This was the first instance I can remember of my being enamored of a mother. Now I'm a total momaholic, but I was twenty at the time and hadn't realized that being a mom is, on its own, fucking sexy.

I paid extra special close attention in her lessons, sat up front, and asked a lot of questions. She probably thought I was retarded. Which, in a way, I was. Whenever I really like a woman, I get nervous around her and stammer and the blood that would normally feed my brain-functions floods my extremities and makes me tingly and mostly useless.

So day in and day out I'd try to manage my love for her and not embarrass either of us too much, and I probably did a passable job. Until she assigned our final project. She asked us all to become experts on a work of art in a Paris museum and then do a hearty, on-site oral report for the class. We were scheduled to visit one or two museums a day at the end of the semester to hear the presentations. The other twelve or so students read up on their painting or sculpture and did a perfectly fine job explaining it to the class. They did normal things like detailing the historical significance of their painting along with the techniques the artist used to create it. I, on the other hand, went bananas.

First off, I got my hair freshly cut and coordinated an outfit to wear, for Madame Royer was an elegant Parisian woman; I didn't think a Robert Parrish jersey and Carhartt jeans would be appropriate attire. I brought my best brown corduroys and a smart V-neck sweater to the dry cleaner days in advance, and under the sweater I wore a blue-and-white-striped French naval-style shirt.

I wanted my outfit to say, *"I'm just your average brilliant, yet totally chilled-out, art historian expounding on nineteenth-century Symbolism. No big deal. Everybody be cool, but feel free to let it all hang out and have sex with me if the need arises."*

I also crawled up the ass of my selected painting, Gustave Moreau's *"Jupiter et Semele,"* and built a research facility.

I lived within walking distance of the Musée Gustave-Moreau, which also used to be Moreau's house and studio, so I was free to study his work with the day-in day-out dedication of a psychopath. And I did! The museum's staff would greet me with increasing familiarity with each visit I made.

"Wow, this kid loves him some Moreau," I imagined them saying in a break room whose walls were adorned with half-finished Moreaus, his warm-up sketches, and maybe a bejeweled water cooler wrapped in a ruby sash—the way he would have wanted it.

When the day for my presentation came, I was in fighting shape. Our class took the metro to the museum and walked around looking at Moreau's cluttered paintings in his cluttered home. Moreau was a Symbolist and most of his paintings are complex depictions of Greek myths, gods, and heroes. His best paintings illustrate one or perhaps two classic stories, but he also painted complex works of ornate imagery that aren't terribly fun to look at but are *ideally* suited to a love-struck student's top-heavy, indigestible presentation designed to impress a married art professor.

When it was time for my presentation, Madame Royer gathered the class in front of the imposing eight-by-four-foot painting of a terrifying Jupiter who had just God-fucked the mortal Semele so hard she had died. Do I know how to pick a painting to impress a woman that I'm in love with? I'd say I do! Looking at the painting now, I can't imagine someone describing it without using the words "scary" and/or "forensic." Dead-eyed Jupiter looks like he might even eat Semele if you look at the painting long enough. Thirty or so attending angels, humans, and who-knows-what-the-fucks stand around averting their eyes, very bummed out about the lovely Semele, mother of Dionysus, who now lies nude and dead across Jupiter's bejeweled lap. He didn't even take his bejeweled robe off to give it to her. Classy.

I dropped a hot load of art-science on the class, picking apart every horrid detail of the story, Moreau, and the Symbolist movement at large, his painting techniques, and when and how he enlarged the painting when he felt it wasn't big and terrifying enough. The class watched, thoroughly weirded-out by how intimately I knew the painting. People shifted uncomfortably as I transparently sublimated my love for our professor into words about a bizarre and impenetrable painting. Some frowned. Madame Royer watched wide-eyed and amazed as I unspooled my knowledge of Moreau, which, at that point, probably even dwarfed that of Moreau's wife and children. When I finished, she actually clapped and said, "Bravo, Robert!" In the U.S., she would've had me placed on a watch list, but in France, being obsessive about anything art-related, no matter how bizarre, is generally viewed as a positive.

I'd like to tell you that we then began an affair with the blessing of her husband, and that I left Paris some months later, promising to return and build a house/museum filled with creepy Moreaus we could grow old in together, but that is in no way what happened. We had one or two short conversations after that, and on the last day of school I told her, *"Votre leçons me manquerais."*

While this story is certainly embarrassing and silly, I think it's important to hurl ourselves at people with whom we have no shot from time to time. It's good to be humiliated. It's good to overreach and fail publicly, especially in romance. It helps us calibrate properly to the interpersonal relationships that are appropriate for us. In Paris, in the spring of 1998, I was better suited to booze-fueled make-out sessions with non-moms in dirty bar bathrooms as we both made an effort not to puke in each other's mouths. That is perhaps the greatest lesson Madame Royer taught me.

une toquade

During my junior year in Paris I tried to travel as much as possible on weekends. France is slightly smaller than Texas, so it was easy to get somewhere thoroughly exotic (to me) with a short flight or train ride.

One morning, after my French political science class, my friend Alan asked me if I wanted to take the train up to Amsterdam with him for a long weekend and stay with a girl he knew. I'd never been to Amsterdam, so I said yes. Alan was another American student. He was around my height, six foot three or so, a first-generation child of German immigrant parents, and he was on the NYU fencing team. He had curly blond hair, an arresting gaze, and was a brash, outspoken, rich premed student whose entitled attitude suggested he'd gotten what he wanted from the day he was born. He talked about anal sex a lot. He liked to fuck women in the butt. He also liked muscular, athletic women with small breasts. In addition, he was extremely homophobic. I will let you draw your own conclusions from my description.

Myself, I've never been a butt fucker. I started to try it a couple of times with a couple of girlfriends, after they'd said, "Sure, let's give it a shot." Pretty quickly into our effort though, they both said, "Ow. I don't want to do this," and that was A-OK with me. I'm of the mind that vaginas are a more than adequate place for me to put my penis and I have just never really had a hankering for ass. I squeeze 'em and bite 'em and spank 'em if necessary, but as far as thinking "I need my penis in there" goes, that doesn't really happen. Probably the only scenario in which I'd be "jazzed" to fuck a woman in the ass is if she was like, "Hi, Rob, I'm an experienced recipient of *le buttcock*. Can you please do something to me that I like very much which is fuck my asshole while I moan and say things like, 'I am enjoying this. Thank you. Thank you for fucking me in my tiny little asshole, you nice man.'" I would fuck that woman's ass and probably like it a lot. But hearing "Ow" during sex is just about the hugest bummer I can imagine, so since I heard it twice from nice women I cared about, that kind of knocked butt fucking off of my wish list, where it had never held a high position anyway.

As far as my own ass goes, I never put anything in there

anymore. I heard it felt good to put a finger up there when you masturbated, so I tried that a few times as a teenager, and it did, indeed, feel good. Now, though, that's too much of a production, plus I'm really not sure how I would explain that to my wife if she walked in and caught me naked with my boner in one hand and my asshole wrapped around the finger of another. I guess I could say, "Fuck you; it feels good. You should try it." Why not? That could be very liberating and open new vistas of sexual honesty in our relationship.

The only other time something was inserted into my b-hole was when a girlfriend tried to put a small vibrator up there while she was blowing me. I did not care for that one bit. I almost cried. So when a woman says she doesn't want a dick up her ass, I am completely sympathetic. Not that I hear "I don't want a dick up my ass" from women a lot; I mean, I'm not going around saying, "Ma'am, that ass of yours . . . may I put my dick up it?" I pretty much almost never say that. Actually, I just thought about it; I've never said that.

Despite the fact that Alan and I never connected on the issue of anal sex, the fact that he had a place to stay for free in Amsterdam was more than enough for me to agree to travel with him. I was as excited to see all the museums and architecture as I was to brazenly eat hash in public and try to make my brain fall out.

When we walked out of the train station in Amsterdam, a beautiful blond girl named Ineke greeted us. She had long, wavy hair and blue-green eyes and she wore a yellow denim coat and a black miniskirt with tights. She had a funny little angular, upturned nose, but that sort of humanized her and made her more beautiful than if she were merely perfect. I liked her right away. Alan had alluded to the fact that they'd met and hooked up a bit in New York the year before. Ineke also referred to her boyfriend occasionally, so I figured I'd just have to be content to look at her, which was fine with me. We left our things at the apartment Ineke shared with her sister and then rode bicycles around Amsterdam and over the canals on bridge after bridge and drank Grolsch and smoked pot. It appeared Alan wasn't making any concerted effort to rekindle the flames of their previous romance. They seemed friendly with each other; nothing more.

Amsterdam was magnificent. The network of canals that runs through the city allows you to be near water all the time, and the prevalence of bicycles over cars means you're filling your lungs with clean air as you meander, so the overall effect is a very satisfying sensorial experience. It just feels good to be there.

On our second day there, we took the train to Leiden and went to the beach. It was autumn and the day was gray and cold. The beach was endless in either direction and the wind stirred up a sandstorm of sorts that was only about two feet high, so you couldn't see your feet through the swirling sand as you walked around. The sand did not, however, reach up anywhere near our faces to impede our breathing or the visibility. It created a mythical environment and I would not have been surprised if a cloaked figure approached me and issued a warning from the underworld or offered me three wishes. As it was,

I did see a person riding a horse in the distance, who may very well have been an intrepid wizard. After taking that timeless scene in, we turned around and saw the only other life-form on the vast beach, a man with his pants around his ankles, shitting onto the beach. Maybe the curious sandstorm swallowed it right up though? I would like to believe that. Or maybe he was American and afraid to shit in a Dutch toilet, because get this: Dutch, German, and Polish (and probably other countries' too) toilets are made so that when you shit, it lands not in water, but on a sort of porcelain "stage," where it stinks up the bathroom much more quickly than if it were protected by an inch or two of water. Only when you flush does merciful water shoot out and coax (most) of your turd down into the bowl and off to wherever the local sewage blasts off to. (Hell? I like to imagine a ghastly waterfall of shit raining down in Hades while goblins and congressmen moan in pain.) I would like to go on record and say that I do not care for European shit-stage toilets. And I'm not being prissy; I actually enjoy shitting into hole-in-the-ground toilets, which you occasionally find in old places in Europe. It feels deliciously natural and healthy to shit in a full squat. It is a far, far more natural position for the body to evacuate waste than the modern comfort thrones we're used to, shit stage or no.

We then explored the city of Leiden, home to the Netherlands' oldest university, where I was shocked to discover students receiving world-class education paid for with tax dollars rather than the mind-numbing *mints* Americans fork over in the form of tuition. That was an eye-opener for twenty-year-old me who'd been raised obliviously on capitalism. Global education payment methods aside, I paid more attention to Ineke than I did to anything else as the day progressed. She was certainly kind to me, but I didn't dare hope that she did it for any reason other than that she was just a nice person.

After a long day, we took the train back to Amsterdam and retired to the apartment that Ineke shared with her sister Rosemarie, and we went to sleep. The phone rang around three in the morning. It was a wrong number, but it woke us all up. As I closed my eyes and sought to resume my dreams, Ineke crawled into my bed rather than hers. She immediately kissed me and began undressing me. We got extraordinarily familiar with each other very quickly, twice. I was in absolute shock because not once ever before (or since) had a beautiful woman whom I'd never even kissed jumped unannounced into my bed and attacked me in such a philanthropic manner. I figured it must mean we were in love and that we would likely get married when the sun came up and she got rid of her boyfriend and I faxed my mom—it was 1997—to tell her I was never returning to the U.S. The next day, however, I gathered my wits slightly and returned to Paris with Alan. Ineke and I planned to see each other again as soon as possible. We immediately began to write letters and talked on the phone fairly frequently.

A few weeks later, Ineke traveled to Paris with her boyfriend, and left him for a few hours to come see me. We walked around Montmartre and then went to the apartment I shared with my eighty-five-year-old roommate, Jacqueline. Jacqueline was, thankfully, asleep.

How I thought this behavior was normal, or at least okay, is beyond me. But I genuinely assumed that we were just starting a life-long love affair in our own unique way. I thought about her all the time and would get a stomachache when I did. I was obviously in some pathetic form of love. At first, Alan had been miffed that I'd hooked up with Ineke under his nose, but he didn't stay mad. I figured I'd found the future Mrs. Rob Delaney, so while people may have been hurt in the process, I chose to believe that sometimes that's just the way the barbed love ball bounces.

A few weeks after Ineke's visit to Paris, I heard that some other guys I knew were planning a weekend to Amsterdam, so I thought I'd join them and visit my blessed Ineke. The two guys I went up with, Bob and Trevor, were American and in another Paris exchange program. Bob, it so happened, I'd grown up with in Massachusetts. Trevor was in some of Bob's classes, and was a relative stranger to me.

We took the train up to Amsterdam on a Thursday. Not long after arriving, we met Ineke at a café. Out of the gate, she and my new friend Trevor began to flirt aggressively. It was egregious. Bob was as uncomfortable with it as someone who was somewhat disinterested could be. I was reeling. I had been *certain* that even though she had a long-term boyfriend and had hooked up with me while a former flame slept a few feet away on the floor, I was *certain* that we were to be wed once she ironed out a few small details. It is fair to say that this feeling evaporated, or perhaps was *cooked* away by the funky heat of Ineke and Trevor's desire for each other. We ate a horribly uncomfortable dinner at an outdoor Italian restaurant, with Trevor and Ineke flirting and exchanging smoldering looks every few seconds and my jaw progressively dropping until it unhinged and parked itself between my shoes on the floor. Afterward, Ineke and Trevor went one way and Bob and I went another. We spent the night in the attic of Bob's friend's cousin, who happened to live in Amsterdam, and took the train back to Paris the next day, without bothering to hook back up with Trevor. Bob was kind and understanding of my frustration, as he knew about the couple of times Ineke and I had fairly recently spent time together without pants on. I was upset, naturally, but I didn't go totally bananas because even in my dejected state I could at least intellectually appreciate that things like devotion or fidelity weren't high on Ineke's list, and I wasn't the guy to inspire them in her. I knew I was entirely responsible for my position. I vowed not to instantly fall in love with and get involved in any more long-distance relationships with beautiful blond Dutch women who had long-term boyfriends and also fooled around with whoever came through town. I had learned my lesson!

I settled back into my routine of classes, reading, and strolling around Paris's parks, museums, bars, and cemeteries, and I didn't grant Ineke too much mental real estate. UNTIL! A couple of weeks after pulling her out of my heart-garden, root and branch, I got a letter from her. In the letter she said she didn't understand why I had seemed upset when she and Trevor had indicated that they wanted to be naked and sweaty together. She also detailed WHY she found Trevor so incredibly attractive, *literally itemizing the different colors she felt she could see in his eyes.* Finally, she said she felt I'd come to Amsterdam the second time with a "hidden agenda." It was an amazing letter. I can understand her urge to formally wrap it up between us, though in my opinion, her actions had done a perfectly thorough job of that.

I grabbed a postcard off my desk and wrote: "Ineke, in your letter you refer to a 'hidden agenda.' My agenda was not hidden at all. In fact it was quite clear: to spend time with a girl I cared about. In any case, you needn't worry, because I will never bother you again." I put a stamp on it and walked out the door to mail it.

As I was about to put the note in the mailbox, I noticed that the back of the postcard had a painting of a dead blond woman floating peacefully in a lake, her hands bound, and a shadowy man standing triumphantly on the bank, admiring his nefarious handiwork. The painting is by Paul Delaroche and it's called *La Jeune Martyre.* Did the woman in the painting look like Ineke? Yes, yes she did. Could an entirely valid alternate title for the painting be *If You Begin a Torrid Romance with a Guy I Introduce You to, Right Under My Nose, I Will Murder You and Throw You in a Lake?* Yes, yes it could have.

I'd bought several of those cards at the Louvre, initially thinking, *"Oh, a pretty lady floating in a pond, who is for some reason wearing a beautiful white dress . . ."* Upon closer examination, I realized her hands were bound and it was just a really excellent, detailed oil painting of a violent crime scene. But, by that time, I'd already bought them and I was going through postcards like crazy. I just figured that my next few messages to family and friends would just be slightly more "murdery" than usual. No biggie.

As soon as I saw that postcard in my hands, I knew that if I sent it to Ineke and she was ever hurt, murdered, or died of natural causes at age ninety-two, I would understandably be arrested. Plus, I may not have "liked" her anymore, but I didn't want to terrify her and make her go into hiding, so I decided not to mail the postcard.

I never saw Ineke or heard from her again. I sincerely hope Trevor never left Amsterdam and he, Ineke, and her boyfriend entered into a polyandric marriage and lived happily ever after, raising kids who couldn't say with one hundred percent certainty which of their dads was their real dad. Unless they had kaleidoscopically beautiful eyes, in which case their dad would be Trevor. Terrific!

vault on a planet your parents had never even heard of? @robdelaney I got my first email address in 1999 to keep in touch with a girl I met in Poland. She's dead now but I still use email. @robdelaney "The holocaust didn't happen, Buzz Aldrin did 9/11 & I wear my mom's panties." - guy who doesn't know how to play 2 Truths & a Lie @robdelaney ME: Tall, dark, toilet-trained. YOU: Pizza. @robdelaney If you throw the candy past the kids, they run after it & you have like 3 seconds to show their mom your dick. @robdelaney NYC followers! If you're in the storms path, I URGE you to send me nude pics before you lose power.

PART V   *la famille*

#safety @robdelaney "I'd like to carpet bomb Iran, literally for fun, & generally ignore the rest of the world, except where I store money." - Mitt Romney @robdelaney For Halloween I'm going as that feeling you get at a store when you try to refold a sweater properly & put it back on the shelf. @robdelaney Pretty awesome that we have a black President. Maybe one day we'll even have a President named Sean. @robdelaney I would rather be a goat or a bag of teeth than a "low information voter." @robdelaney Sephora is my favorite place to fart. @robdelaney 1. You're confined to a hospital bed. 2. You're 11. 3. You sustained brain damage in a car accident. - Reasons to watch shows on "The CW" @robdelaney John Lennon would have been 82 years old today had he not perished on 9/11. #KONY2012 @robdelaney How fun must Columbus, Ohio be on Columbus Day? I bet it's like one big Studio 54. Cocaine & orgies everywhere. Mimes & shit... @robdelaney MISSED CONNECTION: You were "a woman" & I am "lonely." @robdelaney "I was gonna vote for [insert candidate] but after watching the debate I'm going to vote for [that exact same candidate.] - Everyone @robdelaney Not totally sold on astrology, but Libras DEFINITELY hate it when you throw a bucket of paint on their car. @robdelaney It's cute that the NRA thinks guns could defend you from a government that has a high fructose corn syrup nozzle up every citizens' asshole. @robdelaney "One Two Three Four Five Six... KEVIN!!!" - how I would introduce myself 100% of the time if my parents had blessed me with the name Kevin @robdelaney I'm so mad at these refs I'm gonna go to Foot Locker & shit on the floor! @robdelaney Twiter helps me keep my finger on the pulse of what today's youth is jazzing & vibing to. #hip #relevant @robdelaney Cop at the gym just puked when he saw me do squat-thrusts. Said he hadn't seen anything that hateful or violent since

l'hépatite a

In 2010 I was writing on an MTV show called *Ridiculousness*. It didn't win Emmys and it probably wasn't anyone's "favorite" show, but I will suck its figurative dick forever because the moment I joined its staff marked the day I was finally making one hundred percent of my living from comedy. I haven't had a day job since. So if I one day get the face of its host—skateboarder and entrepreneur Rob Dyrdek—tattooed on one of my kids, step off; it's there for a reason.

One day at work, while writing fart jokes for Rob, I started to feel sick. Nothing terrible, just achy and generally misera-ble. I did what I often did in that situation and went to my secret hiding spot to take a nap. My little hideaway was a room that was mostly filled with servers for all the editors' computers. It had a little me-sized area where I could wedge between the servers and sleep on the floor. It was good sleep too, in there. In retrospect, I realize it might have been dangerous to routinely spend an hour or more on the floor of a room filled with whirring machines and questionable ventilation in an old building, but I thought it was cozy. After my nap, I got up and still felt like shit.

At the end of the day, I picked up my wife and we drove to Ojai to spend a romantic weekend that we'd planned.

My wife is a wonderful person, but if we'd planned a trip and my hand got ripped off by an escalator, she'd be like, "Fuck you, put it in a bag and bring it." She would be a terrible nurse and a very good drill sergeant. So I knew that merely being "under the weather" would not get me clearance to stay at home. Our first night in Ojai we went to a nice restaurant and I ordered some food. I don't remember what it was, which is sort of illustrative of the disease I was about to find out I had. I do remember staring at the food and wondering how in fuck I was going to get it inside my body. That was a bad sign, since I can normally eat in any situation. I love to stuff food inside me, ESPECIALLY when I'm away from home and the reptilian fear that I might be stranded away from my personally stocked pantry kicks in and I must just STUFF my body if I want to survive the uncertain times ahead. I couldn't eat. Though Leah was unsympathetic, she was now aware that I was indeed hurting. We went back to our hotel. When we returned to the brightly lit room, Leah gasped.

"You're yellow!" she said. I looked in the bathroom and I was, indeed, yellow. The whites of my eyes were also yellow. It was a yucky yellow too; not an olive or a tan or anything exotic. I called my doctor and told him my symptoms. He thought it might be hepatitis A and that they'd do a blood test on Monday to find out. I did a little homework on the Internet and when I felt certain I wouldn't likely drop dead too soon, we resolved to stay on our little vacation.

Looking in the mirror, I felt dirty. And not a sexy dirty; a dirty dirty. Additionally, my urine was super-heated. I didn't pee on a thermometer to get a reading, but it felt like it was maybe seven hundred degrees. And I was weak. The idea of doing anything was exhausting.

If you'd asked me to hand you an envelope filled with feathers, I would have said, "My apologies; that's just too much for me right now. Please go away."

I also vomited once or twice a day.

What was odd though is that it wasn't an *"Oh my God, I am overwhelmed with a tummy typhoon! I must expel my stomach's contents immediately."* It was more that I could feel poison gradually accumulating in my stomach throughout the day and I'd think, *"I guess I should get rid of this now."* I could, quite literally, "schedule" my pukes.

I went in on Monday and they drew blood. I'd remained yellow, had no appetite, and was puking once or twice a day.

After the visit to the doctor, I foolishly went back to work. As long as I didn't poop in or near anyone's mouth or food, others were fairly safe from infection. I figured I'd soldier through, since all I did was sit in a chair and write jokes.

And then the fun started!

I'd been back at my desk for maybe five minutes before Christian, one of the show's producers, came in and said, "Dude, guess what: Chrissy and Ellen have hepatitis!"

"Oh, wow," I said.

"How did your doctor appointment go?"

"Um, well, I was tested for hepatitis too, and they think that might be what I have."

The tone of the room changed and the four people in it looked at me the way you'd look at a dead crow you'd found on your living room floor.

"Don't worry," I said, "they told me I'm only contagious if you eat my poo. So, um, don't do that and you'll be fine."

Someone found out that Chrissy had been in the hospital for several days. Ellen had been home sick for a week. Then our executive producer came in and announced that his wife had hepatitis. It was an epidemic! Not long after, our executive producer told me to go home and await further instruction. Then my doctor called me to confirm that I did in fact have hepatitis A. He told me I'd just have it until it went away, that there was nothing we could do, and that it might take a couple weeks to start feeling normal. I eventually found out that two other people in our office had contracted it, bringing the grand total up to six.

I called my wife to tell her I sure did have hepatitis A and would have a couple more rough weeks to look forward to. She was much more pleasant once it was confirmed that I had a reasonably serious disease.

All of the women who got hepatitis were really beautiful and I wish I could have gotten the hepatitis from them, or at least have been quarantined with them once we found out we had it. I guess since the only way you can get hepatitis is to eat poop in one form or another, I'd rather have gotten chlamydia from them. Chlamydia! Now there's an STD! It's the only STD I ever got and I didn't even know I had it until a doctor tested me for something else. Then you just take drugs and it goes away. Not that it can't have very real ramifications for women—it absolutely can—it's just nice that if you catch it and treat it early enough, it goes away, unlike AIDS, herpes, or BUTTHOLE WARTS, which stick around for the long run. When I was at the halfway house after rehab, one of my roommates asked me to give him a ride to a health clinic to get his genital warts frozen off. It hadn't occurred to me the type of maintenance one would have to do if they had witchy warts around their junkyard.

In any case, they didn't send me and the sick, sexy women I worked with to a quarantined biosphere in the Arizona desert; they just sent us home to recover individually. Pretty lame if you ask me. I'm surprised I ever truly "healed" emotionally. My wife was at work, so I just stayed in bed for entire days and only got up to vomit periodically.

Your liver very much does not function normally when you

have hepatitis. The symptoms are actually kind of fascinating. First, as I said earlier, my skin was yellow. If you're normally whitish, that's unsettling. The yellowness of my eyes was even more upsetting.

The way you get rid of hepatitis is the best. You poop it out. What's odd is that that's the least unpleasant part of the whole affair. Poops that you associate with sickness are usually awful, carnage-ridden affairs. But with hepatitis, you are producing these claylike, nonoffensive-smelling piles of matter that are more *weird* than anything else. And with each little clay butt-sculpture, more hepatitis exits your body.

Then something amazing happened. The Los Angeles Department of Health swooped in to investigate. Apparently when you're diagnosed with hepatitis, your doctor immediately notifies the D.O.H. I was BLOWN AWAY by how good and thorough these people were at their jobs. They interviewed every employee of our show to figure out where they'd been and what they'd eaten for the last month. I had several conversations and spent a total of about two hours with different doctors and nurses helping them zero in on suspected sources of the disease. It was an almost hypnotic interrogation process where they'd help you relax, then expertly guide you through food and restaurant memories you weren't aware you'd even stored. Though I was never told definitively, we all figured it was probably a cake from a fairly high-end bakery we had all eaten. It had some fruit on it that—we decided—had been watered with dirty water or handled by an employee who had dirty hepatitis poo-hands. It made me realize, *"Hey, how about that? There are amazing government organizations primed and ready to pounce and help fix potentially deadly situations."* It was one of the few times I was happy to have a little bit of my paycheck go to taxes. It turns out the government uses our money to good effect here and there. It makes me think of Ron Paul's popularity and people's tendency to embrace Libertarianism. I just can't imagine a world, or perhaps I should say a United States, where that philosophy would work. There are three hundred million people in the United States. Many good, some bad; but there are a LOT and they represent the poor, the wealthy, every race and creed and profession there is, and a government can form a pretty good lubricant for the engine of society.

Also, MTV was magnificent throughout the whole affair. They paid everyone who missed work due to poo consumption and bought every staff member immune globulin shots. It was my favorite type of problem-solving by a big organization: Acknowledge a problem and deal with it thoroughly and transparently. Big ups to MTV for that one. Maybe they sense their karmic debt to the world for creating *Jersey Shore*, and thereby spreading untold numbers of new, incurable strains of sexually transmitted diseases.

The fantastic news is that we all had hepatitis A, not B or C. Those ones kill you. Hepatitis A rarely kills people and then once it's gone, it's gone and you're immune to it. So if you're test-driving hepatitises, may I recommend hepatitis A? It really is the Cadillac of hepatitises.

I didn't really care that I had hepatitis; while it sucked when you had it, once it went away, you were fine. I was terrified that Leah would get it, however, because she was five months pregnant. Information on whether a pregnant woman could safely be vaccinated and/or receive the immune globulin shot that they recommended for people who'd been exposed was not terribly easy to get. Doctors and nurses contradicted one another and you could tell they were filtering their answer through their "I don't want to get sued"-ometers. Ultimately, we averaged their answers and figured we'd get her treated, the rationale being that it was worth it to ensure her liver's functionality during pregnancy. To help safeguard her, I remained a vigilant bather and hand-washer. I also made sure we didn't share cups or utensils and I took strict care not to poo in her mouth, even at night. We didn't have sex either, which was fine with me since I would have probably thrown up on her and, like many women, Leah hates that.

During the three or so weeks I was symptomatic, I didn't dream at night. I'm normally a vivid dreamer and I am fortunate to remember many of them. When I had hepatitis, however: no dreams. Hepatitis stole my dreams. And what types of dreams did it steal? Dreams about cats, primarily. For the last several years, my dreams have been DOMINATED by cats. I know nothing about dream analysis, nor do I put much faith in what I've heard about dream analysis. But if dreaming about cats means anything, I am "that thing" times a thousand.

In real life, I love cats. I'm not a cat "person." I don't even have a cat. We had a kitten briefly, when I was a boy. Her name was Lava and we gave her to my uncle after our neighbors'

Maine Coon cat attacked her, necessitating surgeries and rendering her terrorized for life. My uncle had a bigger house and yard, and we thought she might have more fun being terrified there.

I love dogs, too, so I don't take a side on the cats vs. dogs battle many of earth's citizens are involved in. That said, I fuckin' love cats. And they love me. In me, they recognize a true friend. They'll run across the street to say hello to me. More than once I've been driving, seen a cat on a sidewalk, stopped and rolled down my window, and the cat's run up and let me reach out my window and pet it. We have an understanding.

When night falls, and I wrap up my day and hop in the sack, I very frequently dream about more cats. Often we're talking and just hanging out, they way cats and dudes do, but just as frequently, I'll be lying on the floor with five or so cats just sitting on my body or, worse yet, I'll be just smooshing my face into a cat's belly and tickling it and trying to wear it like a hat. Why? I don't know. They're just such little fucking cutie pies I want to pet them and play with them and make them happy. Funny, I feel like much more of a weirdo writing about this than I do about showing my naked butthole to a person. Hey, at least I'm not hurting anybody. Especially the cats. They love it. And who are you to judge me? Fuck you, that's who. Leave us alone.

Fortunately I got all my cat dreams back after I shit out all the hepatitis.

Now, I'm happy to say I'm immune to hepatitis A. Not that

I'll go out and deliberately consume a human shit burger, but if I eat one by mistake, I'll be A-OK.

It saddens me that my wife's immunity (or anyone's immunity who gets vaccinated) comes from a shot rather than a month or so of puking, yellow skin, and dreamless sleep. Not that I want them to endure what I did, I just feel that they took the equivalent of an express bus to their position of relative safety, missing out on some truly fascinating neighborhoods of scalding piss and crushing fatigue along the way. I, on the other hand, walked.

la paternité

Since my son Billy is a boy, he came with a penis. We had declined to find out his sex when Leah was pregnant because we wanted to be surprised.

When he came out (of Leah's body, via her vagina) our amazing ob-gyn, Dr. Allyson Gonzalez, held him up and said, "Look what you had!" I had to scrutinize his genitals to realize he had a penis and testicles. Not because they weren't lovely and fully formed and all, but because I was just so in shock that if you'd held a clearly labeled cup of peach yogurt in front of me, I would've needed a full minute to register, *"This is peach yogurt."*

We had previously decided not to circumcise if we had a boy. We did our homework of course, and since the official opinion of the medical community in 2011 was "Do whatever you want," we figured we would not have immediate elective surgery on our baby boy's beautiful little penisette the moment after he was born. I'm not a doctor, or even smart, so do your own research and make your own penis decisions, but since soap is generally accessible as needed these days, we decided we'd teach him good hygiene and let him have one hundred percent of the penis he came into this world with.

The sole argument we could come up with to circumcise him was that I'm circumcised. New-parent books and other parents we spoke to often suggested you "do what the dad did" (or had done to him). But since the cycle of voluntary baby penis laceration must stop somewhere, we figured it would be with us. That said, we've come up with an explanation as to why his penis looks different from mine that we are ready to give him when the time comes.

In all likelihood he'll see my penis when we're showering or I'm showing him how to pee standing up and wonder, "Daddy, why is my penis different-looking from yours?"

Per the plan my wife and I have developed, I'll tell him, "Well, when I was your age, my mommy asked me to put my toys away, and I didn't. So she cut off a portion of my penis. So—put away your toys when Mommy asks." I think that's a good parenting decision.

Since bringing Billy home, I've decided that I like him a lot; I love him, even. This is probably because (head reason) I'm programmed to, and (heart reason) the sight/smell/sound of him is intoxicating and I can't get enough of it. I want to smell him so hard that I smell all the nutrients out of the top of his head and make him stupid.

I want his first words to be "Dad? Stop smelling me."

If you have a kid, you know what I mean. If you don't, you don't. You don't know it if you have a pet, no matter how much of a snuggle muffin your pet may be. I would put my neighbor's cat Dave, whom I love deeply, into a blender and puree him should a situation arise where some modern-day Moriarty told me that doing so would ensure my son's safety. I hope it doesn't come to that, but know that I am prepared for it.

One major thing I realized when he was born is that I am definitely going to die. Of course I knew that on paper prior to his birth, but seeing a human life commence in front of my face drove bone-deep the knowledge that lives must also end, just as thoroughly. For the first few days after he was born I would look at his adorable, smooshed-up little face and think, *"You little cutie pie! You will attend my funeral!"*

At least I hope he does. And I hope that funeral is way, way, way in the future, much further than I'd hoped it would be before I became a father. The way I see it, my new primary function on this earth is simply to die before my son. Hopefully it'll happen as far into the future as possible so he is best prepared to deal with the vicissitudes of life, which can range in pleasurability from eating a fresh key lime pie you made yourself after a rewarding sixty-nine session with a new lover, all the way to having to pay for back surgery with three credit cards because you couldn't afford the COBRA payments on the health insurance you lost when you were laid off from your job as a teacher.

Another thing I've learned firsthand is that moms are more important than dads. Measurably. The baby knows the mom when it comes out; it's been inside her for about forty weeks. The dad is just some guy, albeit a nice one, hopefully. And the baby borrows the mom's immune system as it begins feeding from milk the mother's body makes just for it. But dads are still important. Having assisted my wife during her pregnancy, the birth of our son, and as much as possible over the first years of his life, I'd like to put in writing that a man who gets a woman pregnant and doesn't stick around to help is a sad little cunt.

The argument could be made that mother and child are better off without this cunt-faced, cunty-cunt, non-man hanging around, but I still think he should have his bank account drained twice a month and seventy or so pounds of pig-iron hung around his neck for at least eighteen years. I also endorse him being pelted with human diarrhea eight to ten times a day without warning, so he knows what he's missing. Under no circumstances should he be allowed to smell the baby his lazy load helped create, as it may result in an alchemical reaction where he transforms so quickly into a man who takes responsibility for his orgasms that he dies of a heart attack on the spot.

Perhaps my favorite thing about my son is how much weaker he is than me. The reason for that is that I want to hug and tickle and squeeze and sniff him WAY more than he wants me to. If it were up to him, he'd wriggle away and play with blocks or pretend he was a chicken for half an hour alone in his room.

But he can't, because my strength is vastly superior and I pin him down and snuzzle him and smoosh my face into his stomach and tickle his face with my hair and yell, "BLORP BLORP BLORP!" in his face until I feel like stopping. And he can quite literally do nothing about it. The other day I was lying on our couch reading a book and he climbed up and sat on my head and read his own little book about a magic crayon. And I let him. Only for, like, forty minutes, though.

the LA riots. @robdelaney When you're really angry, instead of saying a filthy curse word, try yelling "Finnegan's Biscuits!" I find it quite satisfying. @robdelaney San Francisco airport has RUG on the floor so I can't "kickslide" my bag around. What an embarrassing failure of a city & its people. @robdelaney On this day in 1776, Amerigo Vespucci held Betsy Ross's hand as she struggled mightily to birth this great nation. @robdelaney Mitt Romney's email password is "Chamomile." @robdelaney 10 years ago today, Canada received its first indoor toilet. @robdelaney I haven't seen Republicans this excited since Ronald Reagan invented AIDS! @robdelaney Facebook has made me hate birthdays more than funerals. @robdelaney "Daddy, may I trouble you to clean a shocking amount of poo off my genitalia?" - if babies could talk @robdelaney Remember when Michael Jackson hung his baby off that balcony as a goof? He's dead now. @robdelaney The Navy should develop something based on "gaydar" that would allow ships & planes to recognize approaching objects. @robdelaney "The club can't even handle me right now." What, like structurally? Should we call an engineer? Evacuate? Please advise. @robdelaney "Sorry I didn't reply to your email Terry, a wolf ripped my hands off... Oh these? Um, I got new hands? Gotta go!" @robdelaney "Can I maim myself with it?" - my toddler's mental checklist before deciding to play with something **@robdelaney My son just announced "I like snacks." I'm off to draft a press release.** @robdelaney "Buttocks! Sexy sexy buttocks! Introduce me to your buttocks! My name is Tony!" - from my new song, "Dusk in Vienna" **@robdelaney ME WATCHING OLYMPIC EVENT: "Holy shit that was amazing!" COMMENTATOR: "Ooh, that was not good at all. He must really be upset with himself."** @robdelaney Stressed? Try this: Picture a lake at dawn. Ducks beginning to stir... Then drink 22 beers & drive your car into a church. **@robdelaney If someone's Twitter picture has 2 or more people in it, I write a letter to my senator.** @robdelaney If your ad has one black person, one white person, one brown person & one Asian person in it, I will not buy your product. **@robdelaney Just saw a great panel at Comic-Con, "How to Talk to a Human Woman."** @robdelaney In certain Eastern cultures, it's considered a grave insult to shit all over the floor in someone's home. **@robdelaney One of my favorite things about raps music is the fun ethnic code words they use for everyday things like money & women. I'm learning a lot!** @robdelaney My dog got hit by a train today & we found out my brother didn't make parole. Talk about a case of the Mondays!! **@robdelaney I bet 2 guys named**

The following essay didn't make sense for the book, but originally appeared on the VICE website and was a "hit" with the all-female crew who worked with me on this book. They wanted it in the book, so here it is. My most explicit and passionate thanks to Julie Grau, Laura Van der Veer, and Maria Braeckel, who helped me address all of my problem areas.

problem areas

Hi everybody! How's it going? If you're a woman, I hope your answer is "I'm fucking starving!" Bikini season will be here before you can say "Jamochachino Surprise," so you better be torturing yourself and focusing your meager intellect and out-of-control emotions on shedding those pounds, girlfriend! I saw an article in a magazine yesterday that highlighted "four problem areas" a woman can have. Are you shitting me? I'm assuming that article was written by a woman, because if you think you've only got four problem areas to worry about, you've gone so deep into the "Red Tent" of feminine insanity you might never come back.

I don't have a dedicated bank of super-servers in rural Washington State to store a giga-list of everything that could be or probably is wrong with your body, so I'll just name a few:

> Saddle bags, upper-arm fat, cottage cheese thighs, midriff-bulge (aka F.U.P.A aka "gunt"), flat chest, asymmetrical breasts, butt-beard, bacne, pit-cheese, cankles, surprise tampon string cameos, eczema, ham spatula, ashy elbows, feet of any kind, hairy knuckles, beef knuckles, uncle's knuckles, vaginal halitosis, bald spots, loaf latch, sideburns, flat-bottom, creeping jimson weed, dowager's hump, treasure trail, Pepperidge Farm, razor bumps, leakage, phantom dangle, and panty dandruff.

I know it wasn't easy to read that list since you likely recognized between twenty-two and seventy items from your very own body. Jesus Christ, that's got to be discouraging. You probably feel like some sort of crippled, cupcake-hunting whale, listlessly bobbing in the ocean off the western coast of Mexico, hoping some merciful Ahab will happen upon you and order his big black Queequeg to hurl a harpoon into your heart, ending it all. (Unless there's some sort of afterlife situation, where women who didn't subject their appearance to enough scrutiny are punished for eternity, which, if we're being honest, is probably exactly what happens.)

"Why me?" I can hear you screaming. Well, if you're not too ashamed to leave the house, head down to your local library and pick up a Bible. You don't have to read too far to get to the part where Eve (the first woman to both perspire AND fart when nervous) pigs out on a massive fruit buffet, angering God. As a result, God calls Eve a "fat bitch," orders her to "put some fucking clothes on" (Genesis 3:16), and decrees that henceforth, all women's bodies will essentially be lumpy torture-machines existing to satisfy men, assuming they can keep their "crazy pussy hair" under control (Genesis 3:20–22).

The Bible is loaded with great advice, and it's important we remember that makeup companies and the media and plastic surgeons are not foisting some made-up idea of what's "beautiful" upon women. These laws come straight from the mouth of Dr. Samuel F. Godburgers Himself, issued as He shrieks across the sky astride His prayer-powered Truth Rocket. And the fantastic news is that God's first "Message to the Ladies" appears in the Old Testament, a text vital to Jews, Christians, and Muslims alike. So don't be acting like you ain't heard, unless maybe you grew up in Asia, subscribing to some religion that dilutes its firepower among 330 million Gods (why so many Gods? With that many Gods, there must be Gods named like, "Rick," or maybe a God of hot turkey sandwiches? Why not?). Or even worse; maybe you were raised in a religion that doesn't even have a God to give a shit about what you look like in a bikini. It sickens me to imagine.

I can hear some of you women disagreeing with me. You think the Bible is a dusty five-thousand-year-old comic book written by men. You believe that today's arbiters of tastes and trends are cash-vacuuming soul murderers who subsist on your fear. And you might even think you can hear the board members of Procter & Gamble and the bearded polygamists who wrote the Bible high-fiving through a hole in the space-time continuum and having a good laugh.

But that would be crazy.

Eric would have an easier time starting a sleepover camp for infants than 2 guys named Sid. @robdelaney "Do you have this in beige?" - old people @robdelaney "Socks... they're like... soft little canoes for your feet." - Don Draper, having a stroke @robdelaney Need special medicine for our son's kidneys but we can't afford it because we bought printer ink last week :(@robdelaney If you don't react when the Dr. hits your knee with the mallet, the Hippocratic Oath says he has to kill you with a shotgun right then. @robdelaney I just "favorited" a picture that a friend posted of a bruise on her thigh, in case you thought the internet wasn't important. @robdelaney It's 2012, aka the future. Don't ask me to print shit out, sign, scan, fax, etc. You're not the CIA. Dial it down, Patty Printsalot. @robdelaney Did you know that you're allowed to pull over a cop on your birthday? Try it! @robdelaney My favorite Spice Girl was Coriander Connie. (She was crushed by a falling air conditioner before their first album came out) @robdelaney I bet Patrick Swayze's "Ghost" ghost & Bruce Willis's "6th Sense" ghost make beautiful pottery together in movie heaven. @robdelaney As a kid, I'd pull a girl's hair to let her know I liked her, but now that I'm older & wiser I simply hit her with my car. @robdelaney NOTHING says "I am batshit, incapable of relationships, bad with money & cannot be trusted" like colored contact lenses. **@robdelaney If a cop busts you with a prostitute, slip an engagement ring on her finger & be like "Joke's on you, bro; we're in love!"** @robdelaney Imagine how hard you'd cry if you found out your mom had been eaten by a wolf WHILE you were chopping onions. @robdelaney 4 out of 5 dentists agree my cousin Sheila is remarkably ugly. **@robdelaney Today's the day I finally get my shit together** @robdelaney I might not be the "best" father in the world, but I'm also bad with money & know how to beat a polygraph. **@robdelaney My brother in law won't go to Hooters with me tonight because his wife is "having a baby." #lame** @robdelaney Condoleeza Rice went by Condoleeza Couscous in college. **@robdelaney Seriously, get off the computer once in a while... smell the roses... volunteer... show your balls to a turtle... make a ham fort...** @robdelaney When I see someone pushing a dog in a stroller I understand why the news is filled with murder. **@robdelaney Mitt Romney help me a black man tried to give me health insurance i am hiding w my family in basement come get us** @robdelaney The thing I love about baseball is that it has all the excitement of football, packed into 162 4 hour games. **@robdelaney "I hate this quilt." - my wife, a person capable of hating a quilt** @robdelaney Just heard a little kid tell his dad he

acknowledgments

OFTEN while writing this book, I said to myself, "This is harder than raising a child." I meant it and I still feel that way. The first draft was a brutal and lonely experience, miles away from a comedy club stage where people respond immediately to what I say.

My most heartfelt thanks goes to my publisher and editor, Julie Grau, who asked me to write this book and whose words were like water to me when I was choking on dust in the desert. You're magic.

Glowing, pulsing, and humming thanks also goes to Laura Van der Veer, who guided me through the trenches with her story savvy and kindness. Without Julie and Laura, this book would be garbage, and I would be in prison in Ecuador, maybe.

Thank you to my beloved manager of five years, Kara Baker, who found me as a misshapen lump of clay in the back room of Rififi and fashioned me into the smooth cog that I am now. You are a legitimate bad-ass and I am grateful we're doing this together.

Thanks too to Dickie Copeland, the person I exchange more emails with than anyone else in my life. You are very good at what you do and let us not forget it was the day you entered my life that things started looking up.

Thank you to Sarah Silverman, whose memoir showed me that it's okay to go deep, acclimate, and then go deeper.

Thank you to Matt Pike and Josh Homme, whose music I listen to before I go on stage and when I write and when I drive and when I cook and when I do everything.

Thank you to Bill Cosby for sitting down with my wife and me and explaining the necessity of placing my family above my career and keeping it there. You are my hero.

Thank you to Teju Cole, Caitlin Moran, and Charles Portis, whose beautiful, vital books I read aloud to my wife as I wrote this one. You made us happy and you made us think. You made me appreciate the incandescent privilege of being able to put a book in people's hands.

Thank you to my dad, who read to me one thousand times as a child and sends me books to this day.

Thank you to my sister Boogums. I've been crazy about you since you were born four years and eleven months after me. I am so proud of the woman you've become. You make everyone you know smile; it's almost weird.

Finally, thank you to my wife Leah. I still am routinely flooded with gratitude that we found each other. You are brilliant and beautiful and I would marry you again right now if I fell into a wormhole or "time-walked" into the past somehow by mistake. You helped me write this book and I am in love with you. Thank you for making our sons, Cantaloupe and Podcast, in your cutie-pie tummy.

B

BLACKFRIARS

To buy any of our books and to find out more
about Blackfriars and Little, Brown, our authors
and titles, as well as events and book club forum,
visit our websites

www.blackfriarsbooks.com
www.littlebrown.co.uk

and follow us on Twitter

@BlackfriarsBook
@LittleBrownUK

To order any Blackfriars titles p & p free in the UK,
please contact our mail order supplier on:

+ 44 (0)1832 737525

Customers not based in the UK should contact
the same number for appropriate postage
and packing costs.